Getting Started In Custom Painted Crankbaits

A Wooden Lure Making Guide

Greg "Doc Lures" Vinall

Published in 2015 by Greg Vinall

Email: support@makewoodenlures.com

Websites: http://makewoodenlures.com

http://woodenlureworkshop.com

http://thecrankbaitmasterclass.com

https://facebook.com/woodenluremaking

Copyright © Greg Vinall

All rights reserved

ISBN 978-0-9942813-0-2

This book is copyright. Except for the purpose of fair reviewing, no part of this publication may be reproduced or transmitted in any form or by any means, electronic or mechanical, including photocopying, scanning, recording, filming or photographing, or any information storage or retrieval systems, without express written permission of the publisher. Persons infringing on copyright are liable to prosecution.

Table of Contents

Table of Contents 1
Acknowledgements 3
Foreword 5
    How Important Is A Paint Job Really? 1
Airbrushing Equipment: A Lure Makers Guide! 3
    Types Of Airbrushes 4
    Other Airbrushing Equipment 7
    Your Workspace 12
    Airbrush Safety 13
    Airbrush Care, Cleaning and Maintenance 13
Choosing Airbrush Paints 17
    Solvent Systems 17
    Airbrush Acrylics 19
    Putting Together A Basic Lure Painting Selection 21
    Expanding Your Color Collection 22
Preparing Wooden Lures For Painting 24
    Sanding 24
    Raw Wood Pre-Treatment 25
    Filling, Priming And Sealing Lure Bodies 35
Basics Of Lure Painting 37
    Getting Used To Your Single Action Airbrush 38
    Getting Used To Your Dual Action Airbrush 39
    General Airbrushing Principles 40
    Sealer And Base Color 41
    Coloring with Opaque Paints 42

Coloring/Shading Using Transparent Paints..43

Using Metallic And Pearlescent Paints 45

Fluorescent Paints...47

Color Shift Paints 48

Blending, Tinting, Toning and Shading..49

Aluminum Base...52

Lure Painting Techniques...55

Masking..55

Stencilling 59

Tips For Painting Speckle, Spots and Spatter 63

Getting a Scale Effect..66

Using Transparent Base 69

Foiled Finishes 70

Water-Slide Transfers 74

Putting Eyes On Lures...75

Clear Coating and Finishing 81

Etex (Envirotex Lite) 81

Devcon 2-Ton 83

Moisture Cure Urethane (MCU) 83

Other Clear Coating Options...85

Putting A New Spin On Lure Painting 88

What Is A Helical Motion Path And Why Is It Important? 89

Building A Rotating Drying Jig 91

Airbrush Troubleshooting..103

Airbrush and Equipment Issues 103

Issues With Paint/Spray Pattern 107

Other Wooden Lure Making Resources 112

Acknowledgements

This book has been the culmination of many years of experimentation and testing. Over those years I've had the pleasure of meeting, teaching or fishing with lure makers from all walks and all corners. Many have contributed to the ideas that I have developed and outlined in this book. I feel honoured and very fortunate that these people have willingly shared so many of their skills and lure making secrets with me.

Particular thanks goes to Steven Keats at the Airbrush Megastore in Adelaide, Australia. Steven is always generous with both his time and his knowledge and has helped immensely with the selection of paints, clear coats and airbrush equipment that have enabled me to achieve the highest quality finish to my painted lures.

Thanks also to colleagues Mick McKay and Chester Emery, two Aussie lure makers and first class gentlemen who took the time to proof the manuscripts and provide feedback into this book.

Finally, my wife Mel and my three beautiful daughters, all of whom have sacrificed so much to enable me to pursue my lure making passion and related businesses and have encouraged me through this journey. I couldn't have achieved what I have without their support.

Foreword

Few things are as therapeutic to me as making my own lures. It doesn't quite compare with a good fishing trip, of course, but, if the weather is bad or time doesn't permit a fishing trip, then lure making is a pretty good substitute. Plus, it makes the next fishing trip that little bit more exciting knowing there will be some new lures in the tackle box.

While carving a piece of wood and turning it into a lure is one thing, painting it beautifully is another thing altogether – a completely different set of skills.

When I first picked up an airbrush I had visions of the immaculate, tournament quality lures I would soon be painting. I had no idea of the months of frustration ahead of me! Eventually I had to concede that it wasn't the airbrush that was the problem - it was me!

You see, I'm a *scientist*, and scientists are not renowned for being creative. The average pre-schooler can draw better than I can (just look at my fridge with my 2 year old daughter's artwork). But there I was, using a tool that even some of the best graphic artists struggle to master.

I now know that mastering the airbrush requires a mixture of knowledge and black magic, but if I can do it, anyone can! And best of all, many of the people I know who paint awesome lures (even better than me) also don't have an artistic bone in their bodies!

These days I can usually do a pretty decent job of painting a lure. And the reason is that I've figured out the mechanics of the airbrush, what solvents to use, how to prepare the lure and the paint correctly, and I've identified ways to make and use templates and so on. I have now developed a system that doesn't hinge on me being a skilled artist!

So what follows is not an encyclopaedia of lure painting. It's not the only way to go about the process. And it's by no means a full, complete and comprehensive guide. What follows is an account of my own personal experience and what works for me in my workshop. And years of teaching other people how to paint lures shows that it works for them too!

How Important Is A Paint Job Really?

As a dedicated (self-taught) lure maker and a professional aquatic scientist I have spent decades figuring out what attracts fish to strike at a lure, often with great aggression and determination.

Is it the sound? Maybe the vibration it emits? Does the lure look to the fish like an easy meal, or maybe an intruder that has stumbled into another fish's territory? Perhaps fish strike out of curiosity, fear, anger or frustration?

In truth it's a combination of all of these factors and the luck or good management of the angler who happened to put the right lure in the right place at just the right time.

What's interesting is that my understanding of the optical properties of water, my research into the anatomical structure of fish eyes and my observations of fish behaviour over years of scientific sampling programs all lead to the same conclusion...... color is often not that important in a lure. And lifelike detail is even less so!

A lot of the time, the color and detail in a paint job aren't even visible to fish.

And yet I continue to toil away at my painting bench, exploring new techniques, mixing new colors, day in and day out, always striving to take my lure painting to that next level. I spend at least as much time painting and finishing my hand-made lures as I do carving, weighting, fitting the through wire, making the rattles and so on.

Why do I do this?

Simple! The appearance of my lures is very important to me, as it is to most lure makers. It's a badge of honor, visible evidence of competence and skill. Most people have no idea the amount of design and work that goes into creating a perfect wooden lure...... but they can spot a slick paint job a mile away.

So if all you want to do is catch awesome fish you don't actually need to worry too much about how your lures look. As long as they are well designed, durable and ruggedly built they'll do the job.

It's a very different story if you're setting up a business making and selling custom wooden lures though. Unless your lures look every bit as good as the thousands of other brands on the market, they're never going to sell – no matter how well they catch fish.

Imagine if Ford brought out a new vehicle that was more fuel efficient, more powerful and safer by a mile than any other car on the road - except that it was shaped like a house brick and was painted matt gray. How would their sales go? The package needs to be complete or it just won't sell.

As a lure making and lure fishing author, how much interest do you think people would have in reading my work if it was filled with photos of lures that look like they've been painted by a pre-schooler? No matter how many fish I could catch on those lures I would have no credibility with my audience.

So whether or not you accept my expert assessment of how fish see lures, you can't deny that a quality hand painted finish on a quality handmade lure is very important to humans.

Of course, there is a one other very good reason for creating fishable art: it's a ton of fun!

Airbrushing Equipment: A Lure Makers Guide!

If you stopped and looked around, airbrushes are everywhere. While they may not be used to manually retouch photographs, they are commonly used in sign painting, temporary tattooing, spray tanning, hot rod painting, model and hobby activities, taxidermy, nail art, theatre/movie makeup, shirt painting and fine art - to name just a few. This myriad of uses means that there are lots of different brands and models available, some being better for lure making than others. Our needs for lure making are relatively simple - we actually don't need the most complex, expensive equipment in order to get great results.

In this chapter I'll give a general overview of airbrushing equipment, with specific reference to those items that I'm intimately familiar with (i.e. the ones I currently use in my workshop). But while I'll talk about the brands and models I use, they're far from the only suitable units, so if you already have an airbrush that works for you, go with it.

The processes that lure makers usually expect from an airbrush are:

- Undercoating and sealing. This usually involves larger volumes of paint, fewer color changes and less precise spraying.
- Spraying base colors can be similar to undercoating, or it can require more precise placement of paint. Often it requires frequent color changes, especially if you are painting single lures or small batches of lures.
- Spraying through stencils requires precise placement of an even mist of paint.
- Fine lines, dots and other freehand features require a higher quality airbrush. This isn't usually an issue for lure makers, since stencils and masks are faster and easier.
- Depending on the paint system, you may want to shoot clear coat through the airbrush, too.

Types Of Airbrushes

Trigger action

There are two types of trigger action of interest to lure makers: single action and dual (or double) action.

Single action airbrushes are cheap and relatively easy to use. When the trigger is depressed, the air flow picks up the paint and sprays it in a fine mist onto the lure. The flow of paint is set before you start spraying and remains fixed until you stop spraying and readjust the settings.

Single action airbrushes are great for painting uniform color onto a lure and can work ok with stencils. Where they become limited is when you want to vary the intensity of color, which is a common requirement for lure painting. They can also make detail painting very slow because you have to continually stop, make adjustments to your paint flow, test some more, make more adjustments and so on.

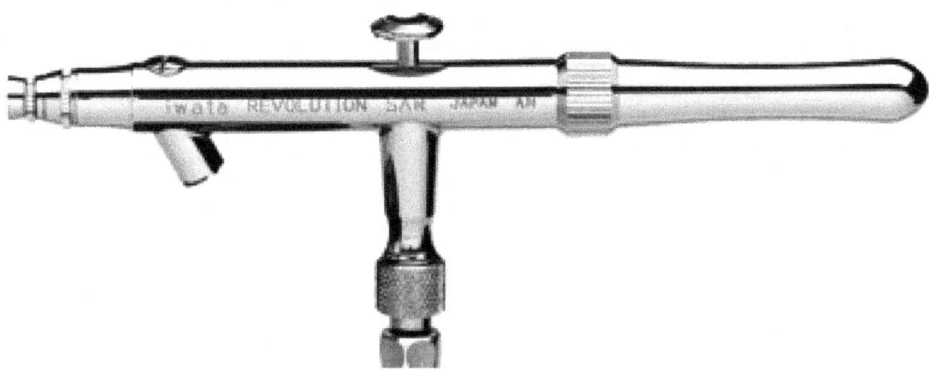

Iwata HP SAR single action airbrush. This is a good choice for spraying large volumes of the same color, such as for priming or sealing lures.

Single action airbrushes are also more prone to 'tip dry', which is when dried paint accumulates on the tip of the airbrush needle and inhibits paint flow. This requires manual removal before you continue painting. Single action airbrushes are a vast improvement on aerosol cans and are satisfactory if you are on a limited budget. But if you can stretch your budget just a little further then I'd certainly recommend you consider a dual action airbrush instead.

Dual action airbrushes have independent control over the air flow and the volume of paint picked up. Depressing the trigger commences the air flow, but unlike the single action airbrush there is no paint in the stream of air until the trigger is pulled backwards. This gives much greater flexibility over paint delivery and reduces spatter at the start and end of the air flow. Because the air can keep flowing even when the paint is stopped, dual action airbrushes are less prone to tip dry, although it's not completely eliminated.

Feed system

The feed system refers to the manner in which paint is fed into the stream of air, and once again there are two options: gravity or siphon feed.

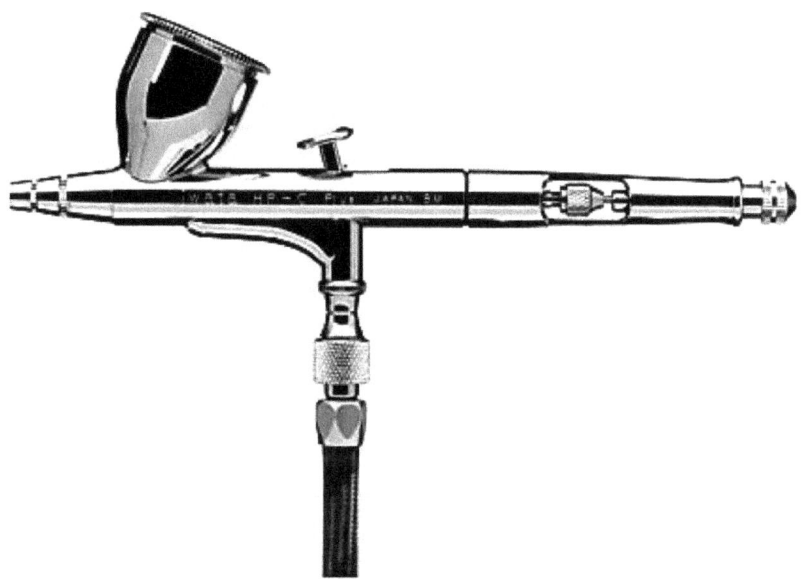

The Iwata HP CP is a good example of a dual action, gravity feed airbrush.

Gravity feed airbrushes have a color cup built into the top of the unit and paint is drawn into the airstream by a combination of suction and gravity. This style of airbrush can operate on lower air pressures and deliver a finer mist with much better control, which is great for fine detail.

Siphon feed airbrushes have a color cup or bottle that attaches either to the bottom or to the side of the unit. In order to pick up the paint and atomise it properly they require slightly higher air pressures than gravity feed airbrushes. But the color cup can be much larger, especially those models that allow a paint bottle to be attached. Color changes are quicker with these airbrushes because you simply remove one color cup or bottle, flush the airbrush and attach another one containing the second color.

Paint Mixing

The paint can be introduced into the airstream either externally, or inside the airbrush.

Internal mix airbrushes give finer atomisation of the paint, which is perfect for grading a color from light to dark, which is often done between the back and the belly of a lure.

External mix airbrushes are better if you are using thicker, more viscous paints.

Suggested Airbrushes For Lure Making

If you aren't constrained by a budget, I'd suggest buying 2 airbrushes that would cover most of your needs:

- A single action, siphon (bottle) feed, internal mix airbrush for quickly sealing and priming batches of lures or for painting multiple lures the same base color.
- A double action, gravity feed, internal mix airbrush with a relatively large color cup, for general color coating, stencil spraying and detail work.

One option is the Paasche VL siphon feed airbrush, which comes with several different tip sizes and a bunch of color cups and bottles. This was actually the first airbrush that I owned and it got me by for a few years, although I did get tired of changing tips all the time. Still, this setup is reasonably priced and isn't a bad option if you don't have an airbrush and are looking for a starter kit.

I've since retired the old Paasche (well, it was "retired hurt", truth be told). I replaced it with an Iwata HP-CP, which is a dual action, internal mix gravity feed unit with a relatively large cup.

I was a little sceptical at first as to whether this one airbrush with one tip size could do everything that I would ask of it, but I was pleasantly surprised! I found the HP-CP can handle my entire lure making tasks, including the fine-line freehand work. I was so impressed with this airbrush that I recently bought a second HP CP so that I can run two colors at once, but that's another story! I can't recommend it highly enough for lure making, and at under $150 at the time of writing it's very well priced for such a quality unit.

The main limitation of the HP-CP (as with all gravity feed brushes) is when you're spraying large batches of lures a base color. In that case, a bottle feed would allow you to have less frequency stops to refill the reservoir.

Other airbrush brands worth trying include the Badger, Aztec and Harder Steenbeck brands. I've played around a little with some Badger airbrushes and found them to be reasonable, but I don't have any experience with the other brands. If you're considering any of these I'd suggest getting onto a few online airbrush forums and seeing what others are saying about them.

Other Airbrushing Equipment

Bottled Air

There are several ways to get the air to your airbrush: you can use cans of propellant, cylinders of compressed air/CO_2, or you can hook it up to a suitable compressor.

I suppose that those small cans of airbrush propellant could be useful for lure making, although I can't honestly think of a time when I'd use them. A 14 oz can retails for $10-15 at the time of writing and will give you an hour or so of airbrushing time. I often spend whole weekends at the painting bench, so while propellant is portable and quiet; it's also the most expensive option.

Compressed air/CO_2 is a more useful option and can be readily obtained from welding and catering suppliers. A 5kg cylinder will give you somewhere around 10 hours of painting time, so it's cheaper than a propellant can, but still relatively expensive.

CO_2 has a couple of advantages: you don't have to worry about oil or water getting into your airstream from a compressor, it's very quiet (great if you are demonstrating or filming) and it's relatively constant pressure.

On the downside, you need to be very careful about using this source indoors, as CO_2 build-up can be deadly in enclosed spaces.

I've heard of folks using car and truck tyre tubes as a source of air. Simply inflate them, hook up your airbrush and away you go. Unlike a CO_2 cylinder (which is fitted with a regulator), the pressure at the airbrush drops off as the tyre deflates, so it's hard to get consistent results. I suppose you could fit a regulator to a tyre tube, but I'm not sure it's worth the trouble!

Airbrush Compressors

With compressors, as with most things, you get what you pay for. In this case though it's not about whether they'll run an airbrush – just about any compressor has the power to do that. It's more about portability, output and most importantly: noise!

If you already own a compressor you will almost certainly be able to just hook up your airbrush and start painting, so the cost will be minimal. The only thing you'll need is a regulator that works down to 5 PSI or so and a water interceptor.

If you don't own a compressor and are looking for a cheap way to get into airbrushing, then any small, cheap tank style compressor is fine. I wouldn't recommend the tankless variety simply because they don't deliver the air at a constant pressure.

The main problem with most compressors is that they are extremely noisy, which limits your painting times to respectable hours. But they do have the advantage that they can run other air tools like larger spray guns, nail guns and so on, making them versatile for those odd jobs around the house.

If you will be painting indoors or late at night (like me) then the best compressors are those that are designed specifically for running airbrushes (surprise!). Again, I prefer models with a tank, which helps to keep the air pressure constant, and I also like the oil-less varieties. These smaller compressors have a few disadvantages, but if you're using them just for airbrushing they are hard to beat.

Noise levels vary between make and model, so if you want something quiet enough that you can use it indoors or at night it pays to do some research. I am currently using an Iwata Smart Jet Plus, which is rather expensive but has paid for itself about a zillion times over.

There are probably cheaper units that will do the same thing, but I haven't used one yet, so I couldn't tell you. Mine is small, portable, lightweight (for a compressor) and surprisingly quiet. In fact, on many occasions I have continued painting into the wee small hours on the patio of my suburban home while my family slept inside. I've never woken them, nor had any complaints from neighbours. That makes the price tag worthwhile in my books!

Spray Booths

In recent years hobbyist spray booths have become cheap and easy to find online. They're a good investment for your lungs if you plan to paint lures for years to come!

For years I used a simple cardboard box as a spray booth. I was working outside and wearing a mask, so I just needed a way to keep the overspray from damaging nearby items. The cardboard box solution worked fine – and it was the right price too!

Eventually I built a spray booth from plywood, with a couple of recycled computer fans in the back to draw the mist away from me as I worked. This worked pretty well, and allowed me to ditch the mask, but the unit was bulky and took up a lot of space. When one of the fans died I was left with a choice – spend time and money building another booth, or buy one off the shelf?

These days airbrushing is such a popular activity that there's been an influx of cheap hobbyist spray booths on the market. I decided it wasn't that much more expensive to buy one, and I'm certainly glad that I did. The unit I bought is big enough for my needs but folds down to a compact size, is not too noisy, effective at removing the paint mist and didn't cost an arm and a leg.

I'm only using airbrush acrylics in my spray booth, and the setup does a really good job of containing the overspray. But be warned: This unit is not suitable for two pack paints, so don't even go there unless you are prepared to suit up, wear gloves and a ventilator! And I'm not sure if the fan motor is brushless, so if you are using flammable paints such as lacquers it would pay to check with the manufacturer before you bought one. None of us wants an explosion.

Other Necessities/Accessories

Regulators: to control the air pressure and deliver constant, uniform air flow at the airbrush you need a regulator. Most airbrush compressors come with a regulator as a standard fitting, but check when you make your purchase just in case you need to order one as an extra. Higher end pressures are in the 20-40 PSI range, but you may want to go as low as 5-10 PSI and still have uniform air flow, so check that your regulator can do this.

Hoses and fittings: each brand has its own fittings for coupling hoses to airbrushes and compressors, so make sure everything is compatible when you purchase your system - or that you can get adaptors to make it all work. Hoses don't always come as standard with all airbrushes, so check whether you need

Airbrushing Equipment: A Lure Makers Guide!

to order this as an extra.

Water and oil interceptors: inline water traps and oil interceptors prevent contaminants from finding their way from the compressor tank to your work, which can avert disasters before they happen.

Airbrush cleaning kit: to maintain your airbrush properly you'll want some small brushes, needles, cleaning solutions and q-tips.

Paint strainer funnels: use these to remove any lumps, dirt etc from your paint and prevent them from blocking the tip of your airbrush.

Airbrush holder: allows you to put your airbrush down when you need both hands. Saves spilled paint or damage to your airbrush.

Cleaning stations: can be handy for catching the spray when you are flushing out excess paint and for rinsing cleaning solution through your airbrush.

Your Workspace

The majority of lure makers don't have a purpose built lure painting studio. So we make use of an attic, basement or maybe a corner in a garage or workshop. Fortunately, that's all we really need! Unless you're turning lure painting into a business you don't need a lot.

Here are the main things to look for in a lure painting workspace:

- **Ventilation.** Even non-toxic paints aren't doing your lungs any favours. Breathing in the finely ground pigments in these paints is still a hazard you don't need. If you're using solvent based paints then ventilation is a heap more important, to prevent health issues and fire risk. Here's the trade off with ventilation though: you don't want your workshop to be too drafty, either! Accurately delivering a fine spray in a crosswind isn't exactly a recipe for success, and keeping slow drying epoxy dust free is a nightmare when there is a breeze!
- **Good light.** Plenty of daylight is the best thing, but if you don't have that in your workspace, or if you plan to paint into the night, you want to make sure you have decent lighting. Ideally, globes, LED's or fluoro tubes should emit light that is very close in color to natural daylight, so you can see how your lures will look in the sun.
- **Comfortable temperature.** Too cold and your paint will take a long time to dry – plus it's just unpleasant. Too warm and the paint will dry on the airbrush tip and you'll struggle to control beads of sweat from spoiling your work.
- **Storage.** Over time you're likely to accumulate a lot of accessories. Airbrushes, paints, stencil materials, masks, clear coats, solvents, jigs and so on. Some shelves, cupboards or drawers will help keep everything organised and accessible, not to mention clean and dust free.
- **Dust free!** Speaking of dust, you want to minimise this as much as possible. Putting your painting bench in your workshop along with bandsaws, lathes, sanders and the like is just asking for your paint job to be spoiled by dust.

Airbrush Safety

Airbrushing is not a particularly hazardous occupation, especially with the paints that are available these days. However there are a few things to consider:

- **Compressed air can be dangerous.** The pressures that reach the airbrush nozzle are pretty low and are unlikely to cause a problem, but be careful if you are working with a large compressor or gas cylinder. These need to be located in a cool, safe place and monitored for leaks etc. Compressor tanks must be drained of liquid regularly and you should wear eye protection any time you are messing with the compressor or any attachments. Always check manufacturer's instructions for safely using a compressor.
- **Always disconnect airbrushes** from the compressor before stripping them down for cleaning etc.
- We'll talk more about paint safety later, but the **airbrush acrylics** used by most lure makers these days are water based. That means they don't contain harsh solvents, are not flammable and are considered non-toxic. However, the pigments in the paint may be mildly toxic and in any case it's never a good thing to inhale paint - so always wear a paper dust mask and/or use a spray booth to avoid exposure.
- While airbrush acrylics have a low toxicity, **urethane paints, lacquers and epoxy clear coats** are much less safe. Be sure to wear gloves, a respirator, and eye protection, work in a well ventilated area and comply with the manufacturer's directions for safe use of chemicals.

Airbrush Care, Cleaning and Maintenance

Cleaning

Keeping an airbrush clean is not particularly difficult, which is interesting given that the vast majority of problems associated with the functioning of an airbrush seem to be due to dry paint somewhere inside the thing. Even the tiniest speck of paint can cause a major problem

Getting Started In Custom Painted Crankbaits

<u>Cleaning between colors</u> should only take a few seconds if you follow a few simple steps:

- Empty the color pot or bottle of any remaining paint and wipe it fairly clean using a lint-free tissue.
- Put a small amount of solvent into the color cup and give it a swirl (I used to use AutoAir brand airbrush cleaner, but now just use alcohol).
- Spray some solvent through the airbrush and while it is spraying lightly tap your finger on the needle cap a couple of times. When you do this the liquid should bubble in the color cup - this is the solvent backwashing in the nozzle and cleaning out any remaining paint.
- Spray the remainder through the brush and replace it with a small amount of fresh solvent. Then repeat the above steps until the solvent runs clear.
- Put the new color into the airbrush and you are ready to recommence painting.
- Try and start with your lighter colors first and work through to the darker ones. It takes a more thorough clean to go from a light color to a darker one.

<u>Cleaning at the end of the day:</u>

- Complete all of the above steps for cleaning between colors.
- Disconnect the airbrush from the air hose.
- Remove the air cap and clean around the needle using a q-tip moistened with solvent. Be extra careful not to bend or damage the needle.
- Half fill the color cup with alcohol and pull the needle back to allow some to run through the airbrush.
- Replace the cap on the color cup and leave the airbrush with the solvent in it.
- For stubborn or really dried on paint, use acetone or thinners instead of alcohol as the cleaning solvent.

You shouldn't have to do too much more than this on a regular basis to keep your airbrush serviceable. However, it doesn't hurt to dismantle it every now and again to give it a thorough clean and inspection.

Airbrushing Equipment: A Lure Makers Guide!

<u>Cleaning after a disaster:</u>

Sooner or later the phone will ring while you're airbrushing, you'll find out there is a hot bite on and you'll run out of the workshop to go fishing (ahh, every fisherman's dream!), or the kids just want you to come and play, now, now, now! The next day you'll come back to find your airbrush full of dried paint. Don't worry, it happens at least once to all of us! Here is how I fix it:

- Remove and discard any paint that is left in the color cup, wipe the cup with a lint free tissue and remove whatever paint you can.
- Dismantle the airbrush as much as you can. Exactly what parts you will have depends on the make and model of airbrush, but generally there are parts in the rear half of the airbrush where paint should never go, so remove those and put them aside.
- If there are o-rings or seals that are not solvent proof (refer to the owner's manual) then remove them, wipe them with a clean cloth and put them aside too.
- What I do from here depends on how bad the situation is. If there isn't too much paint choked up in there and I can get everything apart then I'll fully dismantle the airbrush and put all of the parts that contain any trace of paint into a large jar full of alcohol. I'll leave them there for a couple of hours and will then remove them one piece at a time and clean with q-tips, pipe cleaners and fine brushes. Then I'll reassemble everything, put a drop of airbrush lube on the needle and trigger mechanisms and give it a test run.
- If there are parts that I can't separate or there is stubborn dry paint then I'll use acetone or even thinners instead of alcohol. Sometimes I'll soak it for a while, take the piece out and clean them and then drop them back to soak again if there is still dried paint.
- Repeat until all traces of paint have been removed, then dry the airbrush with a hair dryer, reassemble and you're good to go!

Note: Check with the manufacturer of your particular airbrush before soaking it in any solvent - some airbrushes could be damaged by this treatment. Also, the air valve where the hose joins the airbrush shouldn't be soaked in solvent, nor should any plastic or rubber components such as o-rings.

Maintenance

If you follow the above cleaning procedures then there really isn't a lot of additional maintenance required to keep your airbrush in working order. It's worth having a few spare parts on hand, including a spare needle, o-rings and a nozzle (not always practical).

The two most critical parts of an airbrush are the needle and the nozzle, which are also the two parts that are the most prone to both damage and wear. For your airbrush to work properly the needle must be straight and clean and the nozzle must be perfectly round so the needle creates a snug seal when it's brought forward.

The fine tip of an airbrush needle is especially prone to damage, which is why I recommend having a spare one handy. The nozzle is prone to becoming misshapen as it wears or may even become split.

Cleaning the needle with very fine wet/dry paper (800-1000 grit) can remove any paint build up, give it a new shine and make it move smoothly. Be careful not to remove much metal or you'll be throwing it out and getting a new one! Replacing flat, nicked or perished o-rings and washers is about the only additional maintenance required.

Choosing Airbrush Paints

Airbrushing lures is like fishing - when things are going well it's exhilarating, but when things go pear shaped, you're in a world of pain and frustration.

Having the right tools and equipment is critical for minimising frustration. Using the wrong paint, or combination of paints is just asking for a rough time. And yet, time and again people ask for help with airbrushing problems and when I ask them what paint they are using they'll respond: *"Oh, just some acrylic paint I got from the art shop"*.

Putting the wrong paint through an airbrush is a bit like putting diesel fuel into a Ferrari.

If you really want to get good at painting lures I strongly recommend using proper airbrush paint. Here's why:

- The hole in the tip of an airbrush is tiny and therefore easily blocked. The pigments in airbrush paints are ground exceptionally fine to reduce clogging of the airbrush. The pigments in standard paints are coarser and more prone to blocking the fine nozzle. That means more time spent cleaning and less time painting.
- Paint shot through an airbrush goes on very thin, so the solvent and pigment must be properly formulated to be even, not patchy.
- Paint drying on the tip of the airbrush needle can be a real time wasting nuisance. Airbrush paints and solvents are specially formulated so that this is much less of a problem (although it's not completely eliminated, it will save you a whole lot of time!).
- Using the wrong paint can result in sub standard results, a lot of time pulling down and cleaning out your airbrush and a lack of enjoyment of what should be a very pleasant pursuit.

Solvent Systems

Let me get straight to the point on this: If you're just getting started I strongly suggest that you *don't* go down the line of acrylic lacquers, two pack paints or solvent based systems. All of these have their benefits and advantages, but they also have a lot of drawbacks in terms of toxicity, flammability and/or ease of use.

For the same reasons, I suggest *not* decanting paint from aerosol cans for shooting through an airbrush, which has become a common practice for some artists. Personally, I value my health too much and would prefer to be fishing well into my 90's than dead and buried because I saved a few lousy bucks on paint......

For the recreational lure maker it is very hard to go past water based and waterborne acrylics. These paints have revolutionized not only lure painting, but all kinds of airbrush artistry. They are low toxicity, non flammable, one part, fast drying and easy to use paints - what more could you want?

There is a slight difference between "water based" and "waterborne" paints and even though it's not hugely important from our perspective I'll go ahead and explain it anyway!

Water based paints use water as the solvent in which the pigments are dissolved, so when the water dries, the paint cures with an irreversible chemical reaction that creates a continuous film.

The pigments in waterborne paints don't dissolve easily in water, so they are first dissolved in a mild solvent and then water is added as the carrier for the solvent and pigment. For our purposes it's a subtle difference. The main thing is: neither water based nor waterborne paints use a nasty, toxic or flammable solvent, which means they are very safe and are great for recreational lure makers.

And because of the myriad of uses that these paints can be put to, they are now widely available in a huge range of colors formulated specifically for airbrushing. That means it's easy (but not necessarily cheap) to buy small quantities of a lot of colors. This is important because lure makers generally want a large selection of different colors in small quantities. Of course, you don't need to rush out and buy these all at once, you can get a basic kit and then add colors as you need or can afford to.

The main drawbacks of airbrush acrylics are that they are quite soft and porous, so they need to be finished with some kind of clear coat. You can't get super glossy metallic chrome finishes with this style of paint, which is possible with urethane paints, for example. You can get around this to a large extent by using foiling techniques, which I'll explain more later in this book.

Note: There are iso-free two pack paints available these days, for those who prefer a catalysed paint for greater hardness. Iso (short for isocyanate) is a chemical in the hardener of most 2 pack paints and causes a lot of serious health issues. But don't make the mistake of thinking that iso-free two packs are non-toxic. They still contain a cocktail of solvents and other chemicals that you need to protect yourself from. Personally, for the recreational or semi-professional lure maker I would still strongly recommend using airbrush acrylic.

Airbrush Acrylics

There are a number of brands of airbrush paint to choose from, some of the better known and more popular ones being Createx, AutoAir, Wicked, Golden Artist Colors and Autoborne.

Airbrush paints are kind of like brands of cars - everyone has their favorite that works for them! Personally, I generally use AutoAir for my lure painting because their range of colors is great and I have minimal trouble with tip dry. When something works that well why would I change it? That being said, I have a good mix of Createx and Wicked paints in my collection, and they're great too.

Beware that there are some subtle differences in the solvent systems between these brands, which means that they don't always play nicely together. I've mixed AutoAir and Wicked paints in the color pot with no problems, but have found I can't do this with AutoAir and Createx as the paint thickens in the pot. There is no real problem with spraying one on top of the other though, provided the first coat is properly dried before the next coat is sprayed.

Understanding Airbrush Acrylics and Associated Products

If you're new to airbrushing and you're wondering what colors and associated chemicals you'll need, then this section is for you! Bear in mind that I use AutoAir brand paints (mostly), so the terminology here follows their conventions, but you'll find equivalent products in the ranges of all of the major brands.

Sealer: please, whatever you do, don't skip the sealer! Sealer is formulated to give very strong adhesion to the surface that you're painting. Most lure makers use a white sealer, which gives the color coats vibrancy, however black sealers are also available and can sometimes be useful for achieving different effects. Even over lures hardened with Envirotex Lite (Etex) and titanium dioxide you still need airbrush sealer for the best adhesion.

Opaque colors: also referred to as "semi-opaque". These are intended to cover whatever is underneath them with a new, solid color – although if the bottom color is dark and the top color is light it could take quite a few coats to fully achieve this.

Transparent colors: also sometimes called "candy" or "kandy" colors. These are paints that contain dyes rather than pigments. The advantage is that whatever color is beneath will show through, creating a blend of the two colors. For example, spraying transparent blue over opaque yellow gives green. Transparent colors are fantastic because they allow you to grade from one color to the next in a very controlled way. If you build enough coats of a transparent paint you'll eventually cover over the color beneath, but it takes a lot of coats.

Transparent base: as the name suggests, transparent base is the exactly the same as paint, but without the pigment or dye. It looks like milk when it's first sprayed onto the lure, but dries clear. Do yourself a favor and get some of this stuff – you won't use a real lot of it, but you'll be glad to have it. Transparent base can be used to dilute color without over thinning, for intercoating and for sealing masks to prevent the next color from bleeding under the edges.

Metallic and pearlescent paints: these have very fine flakes of aluminum (metallic) or mica (pearlescent) to give either a metallic or a pearly sheen. For the lure maker there isn't a lot of difference between the two, both are great for lifting the appearance of your lure from ordinary to extraordinary.

Fluorescents: most people would be familiar with fluorescent paints - they convert wavelengths to give themselves a much brighter appearance than they would otherwise have. Great for dirty water or low light fishing! Be warned though that fluorescent paints do have a tendency to lose their brilliance over time as a result of fading by UV.

Aluminum base: is essentially transparent base with a whole lot of very fine aluminum flake in it. This gives an intense flashy base over which you can paint transparent colors for terrific effects. If you have a bottle of metallic base in your kit then you have the option of using any transparent colors you own as metallics. When first laid down it has a brushed metal appearance, which gives transparent colors an awesome sheen and flash. Don't make the mistake of attempting to clear straight over the top of this stuff though.....it turns a dull gray!

Reducers: this stuff is really important! Your airbrush paints need to be significantly thinned to give good results. I know a few guys who use Windex or Isopropyl (rubbing) alcohol for this purpose, but I prefer to stick with the manufacturer's product. Why would I spend so much time and effort making great lures, then risk spoiling the result by using a cheap substitute just to save a couple of bucks? Window cleaner contains lots of other impurities that can affect paint adhesion and curing. And neither substitute has the anti-tip dry qualities of the proper reducer. It's your choice, but I'm pretty settled on mine! Whatever total volume of paint you buy, buy an equal volume of reducer.

Cleaners and restorers: cleaners are used to flush through the airbrush when you're doing a color change or at the end of the day when you are preparing to put the airbrush away. Restorers are used when you accidentally allow paint to dry in the airbrush and need to clean it out (it happens to everyone sooner or later!). I have been using the proprietary chemicals for this until very recently, when I changed to denatured alcohol, which is much cheaper and does a great job of both routine cleaning and restoring. For the latter I dismantle the airbrush and soak it in the alcohol overnight, which softens the paint. Then I get to work with the fine brushes and q-tips to clean everything out before I reassemble it.

Each paint manufacturer has a range of other color and special effects options like iridescent, sparklescent, color shift and so on, but the above are the main ones I use for lure painting.

Putting Together A Basic Lure Painting Selection

The other question I often get asked is "What colors should I start with?"

The answer depends a lot on what colors you want to end up with, but there are some must-haves that I'd recommend you get, and if I was starting from scratch these are exactly what I'd get:

White sealer: I can think of only one occasion where I wouldn't start with sealer....other than that, every lure must start with this, full stop. Get a big bottle so it lasts a while!

Reducer: airbrushes have small openings for the paint to come out, so everything that goes through them needs to be thinned to the right consistency. Have plenty of reducer on hand and don't be tempted to use cheap substitutes.

Opaque white: this is great for spraying over the sealer to give a very strong, white base color on which to spray your base colors, giving a much brighter finish - plus it's great for painting the whites of eyes and the pale bellies of lures and can be used to tint other opaque paints.

Opaque black: so many uses, including spraying outlines, coloring pupils in eyes and creating contrast. And of course shading opaque colors.

Transparent white: perfect for lightening up (tinting) both opaque and transparent colors.

Transparent black: good for darkening (shading) opaque and transparent colors, 3-D scaling, building shadows and other 3D effects, and a ton more uses.

Opaque primary colors: opaque red, yellow and blue can be mixed to give a whole range of different colors and hues, and are also useful colors in their own right.

Transparent primary colors: again, red, yellow and blue can be used to tint, overspray, build color gradations and so on.

The above list of paints is a reasonable starting set because with a little practice you can create whatever colors you need by mixing, blending, tinting, shading, toning and so on. With the exception of metallics and pearls, it covers pretty much anything you might want to do when you are first starting out.

Expanding Your Color Collection

As you become more proficient with your airbrush and painting skills, you'll

Choosing Airbrush Paints

want to increase the range of colors and take advantage of some of the special effects that you can make. Start with all of the above set and then add in:

Pearl white: I use this on 80% of my lures, often giving them a coat of pearl white over the sealer before I start color coating. This just seems to give the top coats a lot more life, especially when I'm using transparent colors.

Aluminum base: I love this stuff for getting a really good, baitfish-like sheen, especially good for saltwater lures, but plenty of freshwater applications too.

Fluorescent yellow, pink and green: great for those ultra-bright lures.

Pearl or metallic greens and blues: perfect for building a striking color on the backs and shoulders of your lure.

Metallic gold, bronze, brass and silver: great for getting that bronzy, earthy appearance, especially for crawfish patterns, or a gold/silver sheen on fish patterns.

Preparing Wooden Lures For Painting

As with pretty much any type of painting, the quality of your finished lure is determined as much by the preparation you do *before* the color coating as it is by your skills with the airbrush. No matter how well you paint, how good your airbrush is or the quality of your paints, if you don't do the preparation properly the results will look shabby. Or they won't last. Or both!

In this section I will give you a brief run-down of some techniques that I use to prepare my wooden lures for painting.

I have several different preparation pathways, and which one I choose depends on how I plan to finish the lure and what quality of finish I need.

Lures for my own use (or for prototypes) usually go through a faster process that results in perfectly serviceable, great looking baits. They are more professional and more durable that half the commercial lures on the market, but not made to my highest standard. My high quality custom lures that are going to be gifts or demonstration lures go through a more rigorous process that is a little more time consuming, but gives a first class, presentation quality lure.

In this section I'll point out where the paths diverge and you can choose whether you need lures that look great and are functional, or whether you want to invest the extra time for a super high quality finish.

Sanding

A lot of people seem to rush into painting their lures before they've sorted out the minor blemishes that occur on most handmade lure bodies. There seems to be some kind of belief that the paint and clear coat will obscure the imperfections. Trust me, they will actually do the opposite!

Ridges, depressions, slivers that have broken away, patches of open grain and other minor flaws will stand out like a beacon on a hill once the clear coat goes on, so if you want professional looking lures these need to be remedied before proceeding to the painting stage.

Preparing Wooden Lures For Painting

I sand my wooden lure bodies down to at least a 240 grit sanding paper during the shaping process. If I'm making them for my own use I may stop sanding at 240, but more often I'll go to a 400 grit paper for a more silky finish.

The two main mistakes that people make during sanding are pressing too hard and being stingy with the sandpaper, and usually the two are related. A fresh piece of sandpaper will remove wood fairly quickly and requires very little pressure to do so. As the paper wears down the particles that do the cutting become dull and the natural tendency is to press the paper harder against the wood. Unfortunately, pressing hard doesn't do you any favours because it results in an uneven surface with grooves and flats where your fingers were pressing, plus it compresses the wood fibre into the lure body, rather than cutting it off.

The remedy is simple: As soon as you notice that you're pressing on the paper to create dust it's time for new paper!

Once I'm done sanding, I will often mist the wood with water and then put it aside for a couple of hours to dry in a warm place. Or I'll wipe off the dust using a paper cloth that has been dampened slightly with water and put the lure aside to dry. Either way, the wood fibres that have been laid down during sanding will stand up and give your lure a sandpaper-like feel. Take a fresh pieces of 400 grit and give the lure one more final light sand.

Raising and removing the grain in this manner prevents it from being raised by the paint or clear, which looks unsightly and is more difficult to remedy.

Raw Wood Pre-Treatment

Spraying any kind of paint directly onto raw wood not only wastes a lot of paint (it soaks into the wood), it also gives you an inferior result both aesthetically and in terms of the durability of the paint job.

Pre-treating your wood is important for 5 reasons:

1. <u>Waterproofing</u>

Weird as it may seem, water is the enemy of wooden lures!

Getting Started In Custom Painted Crankbaits

Dry, unsealed timber acts like a sponge when you place it in water. It's not long before the moisture is drawn by capillary action through the lure, creating waterlogging.

Waterlogging kills lure action fast, especially floating or suspending cranks and jerks. Absorbed water usually renders a lure too heavy or too unbalanced to swim properly.

To rub in some salt, getting moisture trapped beneath the paint is the fastest way to cause the paint to fail. Water expands and vaporises if it gets warmed up, pushing the paint away from the timber.

If your lures are designed to be fished (not hung on a wall), then the paint is bound to get damaged by teeth, abraded by rocks, smacked into pylons or a million other normal fishing events, allowing water to come in contact with the wood. Waterproofing the wood allows the lure to keep working, even if the paint looks well used.

2. Durability

There's nothing worse than painstakingly carving a lure, lovingly painting it and then getting a dent in it the very first time you use it (unless of course that dent is caused by a large fish dangling off the end of it!).

The very best timbers for making lures are often the lightweight ones, especially if you are making crankbaits, surface walkers, poppers and so on. But unfortunately, lightweight timber also tends to be very easily dented. Balsa is a classic example, great for lure making, but you can make a pretty deep dent in it just using your thumbnail. Sharp teeth quickly chop it to pieces.

Part of the treatment process is to harden the wood up so it's tougher and more resistant to dents and tooth punctures. This step keeps your lures working much longer and is one of the invisible differences between professional quality and backyard amateur lures.

3. Gap Filling

Wood is a natural substance, which means that it's imperfect. By the time a lure is fully painted and clear coated, minor flaws like open wood grain can look like the Grand Canyon. It doesn't affect their fish catching ability, but it certainly detracts from their appearance!

Plus, if you're a fat fingered clown like me you're bound to leave the odd tool mark, sanding scratch or other flaw in a lure body.

Repairing, covering, mending or hiding these minor blemishes is all part of the pre-treatment step. If you plan to sell lures for profit, this step can actually save sanding time and get the lure ready for paint faster.

4. <u>Locking In Tannin</u>

Some timbers such as cedar naturally contain a group of chemicals known as tannins. You've probably heard of tannin-stained water, which looks like dark tea. It's the same group of chemicals.

Tannins have a nasty habit of mobilising after you've painted your lures and leaching through acrylic paints to cause ugly brown splotches. It doesn't happen every time and it usually doesn't show up until you've finished painting and clear coating, sometimes days or weeks later!

If you know that you're using a timber where this could be a problem then it makes sense to pre-treat the wood to prevent it.

5. <u>Paint Adhesion</u>

Spraying or brushing paint directly onto a raw wood surface isn't such a great idea. For starters, it will take quite a lot of coats before the paint doesn't soak in anymore and you build up a solid base. Plus, the quality of the paint job will be poor, and if you are using waterbased paints, the moisture will cause the wood fibre to stand up and give a rough, sandpaper like surface to your lure. Not cool.

Preparing your lures properly for painting will not only prevent this from happening, it will give the paint the perfect surface for maximum adhesion and longevity.

After all, if you're going to go to all of the trouble to paint a wooden lure to perfection, you want it to last!

Getting Started In Custom Painted Crankbaits

If you want to create an argument, put a dozen lure makers in a room and ask them to agree on the best way to prepare a wooden lure body for painting!

The correct answer is that there is no correct answer! In my workshop I use several different approaches to preparing raw wood for painting. Some work better for some applications. Others work better for other applications. Which one I choose depends on the wood I'm using, the quality of finish I require and how fast I need to get the job done!

In this section I'll walk you through 4 options for treating raw wood and leave it for you to decide which one suits your needs!

Three of the four main options for sealing and hardening raw wooden lure bodies: penetrating wood hardener, super glue and epoxy (e.g. Etex).

Option 1: Super Glue

Lure makers are funny creatures. Quite often we'll to use household materials to do things cheaply, when better materials are available...... and are often cheaper in the long run!

Using super glue to harden and seal raw wood is a good example. It's a lure making trick that's been around for a fair while, because it's simple and it works...... plus it doesn't require any hard to get materials.

The super glue preparation method is very popular with makers of balsa wood lures, especially balsa wood crankbaits.

Super glue (cyanoacrylate) is watery thin and soaks deep into the timber before setting rock hard. Once there, it waterproofs, seals and hardens the wood.

The easiest way to apply super glue to raw wood is to empty a tube of the stuff into a disposable shot glass and then brush it liberally all over the lure using a small disposable brush. It's a messy task and it's common to finish up with the brush or the lure (or both) glued to your fingers in the process!

Once coated, hang your lures to dry thoroughly. You may wish to apply another coat or two of the super glue to get a really good surface on which to paint.

After the final super glue application I recommend leaving your lures to hang for at least 1 week before going on to the next step. It's important not to rush the painting process as many of the problems you'll encounter will be because of incompatible chemicals that react to create a mess. It's usually the solvents that cause the issues. By leaving it for a week all traces of solvent are allowed to dissipate, which greatly reduces the issues.

You'll find that the process of coating your lure with super glue will cause the grain to raise, which will leave the wood feeling like sandpaper. All you need to do before painting is give it a wet sand with 400 grit paper to remove the raised fiber. The good news is that you need only do this one time. Once the grain has been sanded back it won't raise up again on subsequent coats of glue or paint.

If you are making a through wire lure, crankbait or other style of lure that includes diving lip slots, rattle/weight holes or fixtures, it's a good idea to do the superglue treatment before the hardware has been installed. By doing this, you seal and harden the wood around those fixtures, preventing moisture from getting in later.

If there is a disadvantage to using super glue for this purpose it would be that super glue neither fills gaps and flaws, nor does it lock tannins in and prevent them from spoiling your paint job, should you be working with timbers that contain tannin. It just means that there is an extra step required before painting.

Option 2: Penetrating Wood Hardener

Products such as Minwax High Performance, PC Petrifier or Earl's Penetrating Wood Hardener can be an easy way to improve the hardness and durability of your lures. They are designed for restoring strength to rotted timber in building projects, but they do wonders for timber that isn't rotten!

Penetrating wood hardener is great for making your lure bodies tough and more resistant to knocks, abrasion and even fish teeth! Plus, it's easier to use than super glue!

I use wood hardener after the lure body has been shaped and sanded but before things like through wires and diving lips are fitted. This allows the liquid to get into all of the slots, grooves, holes and so on and really penetrate the wood fibre. Rather than brush it on, I like to dunk my lures in, put a weight on them and leave them for an hour or two. This allows the liquid to soak right into the wood, particularly end grain and areas where water might penetrate later (i.e. where hardware will be inserted).

Once the lures are out of the hardener I put them in a warm, dry place for at least a couple of days, preferably a week. This may seem excessive given the label on the can says that the hardener dries in a couple of hours, but because the hardener has penetrated deep into the wood it takes a while for all of that moisture to come out. Being exposed to air, the hardener at the surface dries first and traps the liquid underneath, so give it plenty of time to find its way back out. Moisture beneath the clear coat is the number one reason why paint on lures will fail.

Once dry, wet sand the lure bodies with 400 grit paper to remove raised grain. You may find that you need to open up the slots and holes in the lure body after hardening, as they tend to tighten up a little!

As with super glue, penetrating wood hardeners don't really help much when it comes to gap filling, hiding grain or locking in tannin, so there will be an extra step required, which we'll address shortly.

Option 3: Propionate

This is one of the fastest, cheapest and most efficient ways to seal, waterproof and harden wooden lure bodies. I suppose that explains why so many professional and semi-professional lure makers use it! It's a lot cleaner and simpler than super glue, too.

Propionate (or more correctly "cellulose acetate propionate") is a clear, plastic-like material that dissolves in acetone. You can buy propionate pellets online through sources like EBay and Amazon. Acetone is of course available at most hardware or paint supply stores, and the only other thing you'll need are some wide-mouthed glass jars that are big enough for you to dunk a lure in.

I use a two stage process for treating lures with propionate: The first step uses a thin solution that soaks deep into the wood and dries hard to make the wood tough and waterproof. The second stage uses a thicker solution that builds up a tough waterproof coat and gives a great surface for the paint to bond onto.

Here's a quick rundown on how I do it:

1. Make a thin solution by dissolving 1 part propionate pellets in 12 parts acetone. If you just place them in the jar and pour the acetone on top the pellets can take a couple of days to dissolve, even if you give the solution a swirl once or twice a day. Grinding the pellets through a mincer, coffee grinder or the like (i.e. ones that you are not using in the kitchen!) will reduce the size and make dissolving them much faster. Remember that acetone is volatile and flammable, so you need to keep the container airtight (wide-mouthed Mason jars with the rubber seal removed are a pretty good option). This solution should be quite thin and watery.
2. Make a thicker solution in a second jar by dissolving 1 part propionate in 6 parts of acetone. This one should be quite a bit thicker and more syrupy.
3. Submerge the lure bodies in the thin solution for 30-40 minutes, remove, slide some blotting paper through the slots to remove excess propionate and let dry for at least 30 minutes, or until the smell is

gone. This should raise the grain and make the wood feel sandpapery, so wet sand it with 400 grit paper, then wipe it dry.
4. Dip the lure into the thin propionate for a second time, swirl it around and let it dry again (this time should only take a few minutes – don't forget to clear the excess out of the slots using blotting paper).
5. Next I repeat this process 5-6 times using the thicker propionate solution, allowing it to dry for a few minutes between coats.

If all goes well the propionate should have filled most minor flaws like wood grain and tool marks and you should have a tough, very clear, glossy surface. If there is a little humidity the propionate can turn slightly cloudy, which doesn't affect the performance but can be fixed by wiping gently with a soft cloth moistened with acetone if you wish. I don't bother.

Many people will go right ahead and paint their lures from this stage, but I prefer to let them sit for a least a few days and preferably a week or so before painting. Propionate hardens when the solvent (acetone) evaporates off, rather than by chemical reaction. And since I apply a lot of coats it's possible for the surface to skin over and trap some acetone underneath. Giving them plenty of time to dry not only ensures that the propionate reaches full hardness, but also that the acetone won't react badly with whatever paint system you use.

One of the down-sides of propionate is that it isn't very effective at blocking tannins from leaching through and spoiling acrylic paints, so you need to add an extra step, which we'll talk about in a moment!

Option 4: Etex

Hardening with Etex (Envirotex Lite) is messier and more time consuming than using penetrating wood hardener, but it is well worth the effort for your "top shelf" lures. For some timbers (e.g. cedar) that contain tannins, Etex can actually be faster than the previous 3 options. This is because Etex is very effective at sealing in tannin, so it's a one step process, where the other options require a second step.

Unlike the penetrating wood hardener, I apply Etex after the through wire has been fitted, because I find that it helps me to cover minor flaws along glue lines and so on. My process is a little involved, but has worked for me for years.

Preparing Wooden Lures For Painting

1. Start by putting your bottles of Etex someplace warm. Be careful not to get them too hot as you may melt the bottle or cause the liquid to expand and split the bottles. I've found that 120°F (approximately 50°C) is a good temperature and I usually put my resin under a heat lamp to achieve this. I know some guys that warm their resin in the microwave after they've mixed it, but I wouldn't recommend this unless you have a dedicated microwave. Putting chemicals anywhere you'll be cooking food later is very uncool and could be a health risk.
The purpose of warming the resin is to make it thinner and runnier, so that it can penetrate into the wood better. This gives greater strength and better water proofing.

2. Next I put my lures in the oven at 120°F (approximately 50°C). The glues and resins I use to assemble the lures are always fully cured and have been given at least a couple of days before baking, so there isn't any odour or health hazard. But to be safe and ensure that the family roast doesn't taste like epoxy, I always place them in a zip-lock plastic bag before popping them in the oven. Don't go above 120°F (50°C) or you may start to soften epoxy resins, split the wood or melt the zip-locks.
Baking your lures in this manner will expand the fibres and open the pores in the wood, which makes it really easy for the Etex to penetrate deeply. As they cool the Etex gets drawn in deep, seriously hardening and waterproofing the wood.

3. Next I mix my Etex up, usually only making 4-5 ml at a time. I thin the resin with denatured alcohol (methylated spirit), which further improves penetration into the wood. So for a batch of 5-6 lure bodies I would mix 2ml Etex Part A with 2ml Etex Part B until I was confident that the two parts were fully combined. Then I add 2ml denatured alcohol and mix again until the solution is consistent.

4. Applying the Etex to the lure bodies is simply a matter of taking them from the oven one at a time, brushing liberally with Etex, being careful to get the liquid into every nook and cranny and then putting them somewhere to dry (NOT the oven!). Leave each lure in the oven

Getting Started In Custom Painted Crankbaits

right up until you apply the resin, which will maximise the penetration of Etex. I use a small disposable brush, which saves clean up time later.

5. Depending on how long the resin remains workable I'll go back several times over the next 30-60 minutes and apply more Etex to any part of the lure that isn't saturated - you'll identify these areas because the resin will have soaked right in and the surface will have a matt finish. Anywhere the surface is glossy is already saturated and if you add more resin to these areas it probably won't soak in.

6. At this point I used to wipe away the excess resin with a lint free cloth to save on sanding, then let the lure harden. But recently I've added another step that speeds up the preparation process and leaves me with a perfect surface to paint. Here's what I do: I prepare a second batch of Etex and once it is thoroughly mixed I add titanium dioxide powder to the resin, a little bit at a time, until I have a bright white mixture.

7. I paint this mixture onto the lure while the first Etex coat is still wet, laying it on quite thick. Then I put the lures on my rotating drying rack to cure (we'll make one of these later). The two coats of resin bond chemically as well as mechanically, giving a really tough exterior.
8. I put the lures somewhere warm and dry and let the resin fully cure for at least 2-3 days, preferably longer, before wet sanding with 400 grit paper until I have a smooth, hard, matt white surface.

This process not only hardens and waterproofs the wood more effectively than any of the other options (in my opinion), it also fills grain and imperfections, seals in tannins and gives a superior painting surface that reduces the amount of airbrush paint required to get full coverage.

If you've decided the Etex preparation option is for you, then you can skip the Filling, Priming And Sealing section and can go straight on to painting!

Filling, Priming And Sealing Lure Bodies

Hardened, sealed, filled, waterproofed and primed, this lure body is ready for painting.

If you've used Etex to harden and seal your wood you can usually skip this step and go straight on to painting. If you've used any of the other options you may need to complete another step or two before you start to paint.

Wood is a natural product and hand shaping wood is not a perfect art, so it's quite likely that at the end of the hardening process you might see open grain, small cranks, scratches or other imperfections. These won't affect the performance of the lure and now that you've hardened it they won't let any water get in, but they can spoil what might otherwise be a perfect finish.

Usually these imperfections are too minor for something like epoxy body filler to be effective - you can put it on, but it will usually rub out when you try and sand it because it can't get enough of a grip in a shallow depression.

If filling is necessary, I generally go one of three ways:

- Apply a couple of coats of oil based, 3-in-1 primer/sealer/ undercoat either using an aerosol or a single coat from a tin that has been thinned down with

Getting Started In Custom Painted Crankbaits

1 part mineral turpentine and 5 parts paint. Let this dry for a day and then wet sand with 600 grit sand paper until the surface is completely flawless.

- I use oil based paint for this because I've found it sticks much more tenaciously to the lure body, sets really hard and sands much better than the water based equivalent. The down side is that it takes a while for the solvent to dissipate from oil paints, so I normally leave it at least a full week before I start painting.
- Because the oil based sealers trap in tannins and oils, this is a good follow up step to penetrating wood hardener for timbers like cedar that have a habit of developing brown stains in acrylic paints.
- I will sometimes use aerosol spray putty such as Rust Oleum Filler Primer or Plastic Primer. I've also had good results using Septome High Build Plastic Primer.
- These spray putties are volatile solvent based paints and dry fairly quickly, so they have the advantage that you don't need to leave them for too long. 24 hours is usually enough before you start color coating, but you can wet sand the filler/primer with 600 grit sand paper just an hour or two after spraying.
- For lures that I plan to clear coat later with Moisture Cure Urethane (MCU), I like to avoid solvents (MCU doesn't play nicely with them) so I'll simply apply another coat of Etex, thinned 50:50 with denatured alcohol. Actually, you can use this option no matter which process you follow from here on because Etex generally plays nicely with everything. The only downside is that Etex is very tough and sanding it is hard work - you need to remove all traces of gloss before you start painting, which is time consuming. I wet sand using 250 and 400 grit sand paper for this process.

Irrespective of how I have prepared my lures up to this point or how I will go about finishing them, my next move is to seal them with AutoAir sealer. Normally I use the light colored sealer, but sometimes I'll use the dark sealer if it suits what I'm doing. Obviously the other brands have their equivalent products, so use the one that's appropriate to your brand, just don't skip the sealer!

Basics Of Lure Painting

Finally, we're going to pick up our airbrush and start painting our lures!

Notes:
- Because I use (and recommend) AutoAir products almost exclusively these days, everything from here on will refer to their range of colors, bases and so on. If you are using a different brand of airbrush paint, that's fine. The painting principles and techniques are exactly the same and the other brands have equivalent colors and products as AutoAir, so just substitute as necessary!
- The amount of thinning and the air pressures I suggest are what I use with AutoAir paints and my Iwata airbrushes (mostly the HP-CP model). They are indicative only and you may need to alter the ratio of paint to reducer or change the air pressures to suit your particular equipment and paints. If you are following what I suggest here and are getting poor results then STOP! Go to the troubleshooting section at the end of this book to find what changes you need to make and simply adjust your settings!

Everything we have done until now has prepared you and your lures for the painting process, now you just need to know how get the best from your airbrush and then practice and experiment until it all comes together and you're painting like a pro!

If you take a look around on Google and YouTube you'll find tons of great info about using an airbrush. The trouble is, most of it applies to artists and a lot of it is irrelevant to lure painters!

Airbrushing lures is usually more about having a system and using it than it is about artistic ability.

So you'll often find that the airbrush tutorials will talk about learning to make small dots, fine lines and "dagger strokes", which are the basic skills you need to create one-off, hand painted airbrush art. But as lure makers we don't usually want works of art, we want to be able to replicate a design quickly and easily onto a number of lures.

I can paint dots. I'm ok at fine lines. But to this day I'm still lousy at dagger strokes, because it's just not important for what I do! But as you'll see, you don't need to waste hours practicing daggers!

Getting Used To Your Single Action Airbrush

Single action airbrushes are simple to use, but rather limited in what you can achieve with them. They are best used when you are spraying a solid color, such as priming/sealing, base colors and basic stencil work. They are also quite good for spraying lines of uniform thickness. They're not so good for detail painting or shading.

Start by thinning your paint to the consistency of milk. Then set your air pressure at around 20-25 PSI for starters. Hold your airbrush between your index finger and thumb, as you would a pen. Your index finger should be resting comfortably on the trigger. Now press the trigger down and use the paint flow adjustment knob (this is often at the back of the airbrush for internal mix versions) to start the paint flow.

Hold the airbrush at working distance from a piece of paper and play around with the paint flow until you get a good coverage on the paper. If the spray looks a little grainy you can try either upping the air pressure a little bit or thinning the paint a little more.

Make a couple of passes over the test paper, keeping the airbrush perpendicular to the paper. In other words, move your whole arm, don't just bend at the wrist. If you are doing everything right, you should get a couple of uniform bands of color across the page.

Now move the airbrush closer to the paper and repeat the process and you should find that the bands of paint are narrower and darker. Do it again holding the airbrush back a little and you should get wider bands that are less intensely colored.

You may need to adjust the air flow down when you are holding the brush close, or move the airbrush more quickly. Otherwise the jet of air can cause the paint to run. If reducing the air pressure causes the paint to become grainy then you'll need to thin your paint a little more. Conversely, when you are holding the brush back away from the work you might want to up the air pressure and paint flow to increase the coverage.

Now play around a little more with your settings. If you'd like to try painting fine lines then drop the air pressure right down to 5-10 PSI and hold the airbrush very close to the work. Try making dots, lines and shapes until you get a feel for the airbrush.

Now you're ready to start painting some lures.

Getting Used To Your Dual Action Airbrush

The technique for using a dual action airbrush is similar to the single action airbrush. However, with dual action airbrushes both the paint flow and the air flow are controlled from the trigger, which gives infinitely more control over paint delivery. It means that you can adjust your paint delivery "on the fly", making it really easy to paint lines of different thicknesses. It also makes shading and graduating colors into each other a snap.

Start with well reduced paint and about 20-25 PSI of air pressure. As with the single action airbrush, the air pressure is adjusted at the compressor regulator as well as at the trigger. So if your paint is coming through a little grainy you can either bump up the air pressure a little, or thin the paint more. Either one will work.

When you use a dual action airbrush you should develop the habit of having the air flowing at all times and just rocking the trigger back and forth to start and stop the paint flow. Depress the trigger fully and you will create air flow, but there will be no paint in the airstream. If you gently rock the trigger backwards you'll start to see paint deposited on your test paper.

Working the brush in this way will go a long way towards reducing the spatter that often occurs when the airflow is started and stopped, but it will also reduce the problem of "tip dry", where a tiny blob of paint dries on the tip of the airbrush and causes grainy or spattering paint flow. Tip dry is normal with acrylics and usually can't be completely eliminated, which means you need to stop painting periodically and remove paint form the needle tip.

If you're used to a single action airbrush, you should be starting to spot the advantages of the dual action already. Painting spots, for example, is much cleaner, because you can get the air flowing and then slowly introduce paint in a controlled way – there are no spatter issues. Shading is easily achieved without stopping, by simply adjusting the paint flow on the fly.

General Airbrushing Principles

1. It's much better to thin your paint too much rather than too little. Thinned paint flows on smoother and gives a lot more control over the delivery.
2. Don't muck about using Windex or other substitutes to thin your paints. It really doesn't cost much more to use the proper paint reducer and it avoids a whole bunch of potential problems.
3. Many light coats build even color and give a much better result than a couple of heavy coats, which can look patchy and uneven.
4. When using a double action airbrush, keep the air flowing constantly, even when the paint is not flowing.
5. To evenly coat a lure, the airbrush must be moving before the paint starts flowing. Keep it a constant distance from the work piece and move your whole arm, rather than just bend at the wrist.
6. When possible, start with the lightest color first. This not only makes it easier to get good coverage of the lures, it also makes switching colors quicker and easier, with reduced cleaning and flushing.
7. Use masks such as tape when you want sharp edges or lines in your painting. Use stencils when you want a softer edge. The further above the lure you hold the stencil the softer and more blurry the edge will be.
8. Reduce your pressure and spray multiple light coats when you are using stencils and masks. This helps reduce the chance of paint being pushed under the stencil where you don't want it. Use the minimum pressure you require to keep the paint atomising properly.
9. Heat set airbrush acrylics between coats to prevent solvents getting trapped and to cross link the paint. You don't have to understand how

this works, just know that if you heat treat between coats you'll get a much tougher finish. No amount of drying at room temperature will achieve the same result.

10 I've found that any time I change colors, paint types or settings, I get best results if the first coat after the change is a super thin, lightly misted coat. Once that coat has been heat set, the following coats seem to lay down much better with less chance of runs or dags.

11 If spatter is going to happen, it usually occurs just as the air is turned on or off (especially with single action airbrushes). Be sure the airbrush is pointed away from your lure when you start and end the paint flow, or for detail painting use a dual action airbrush and start the air flow before pointing it at the lure.

Sealer And Base Color

I can only think of one instance where I wouldn't paint my lures with at least a couple of coats of acrylic sealer before I started shooting color coats - and we'll talk about that later! For every other situation it's important to lay down some sealer and heat set it with a hair dryer or heat gun before you start color coating. If you skip the sealer and go straight to color coating you run the risk of poor paint adhesion and a shorter life expectancy for your paint job.

For efficiency, I normally seal lures in batches, so at the start of a session I'll prepare enough paint for a batch by reducing and filtering it, and then put it in an airtight jar or bottle to use as I need it. I usually find that I get best results by first dusting each lure once or twice with just enough sealer that I can barely see it's been sprayed. Then I'll lay down 2-4 good coats of sealer, being careful to get an even coverage without excessively wetting the lure. I give each lure a blast with a hair dryer to heat set the paint before moving on to the next coat.

Sometimes when I've laid down 4 coats of sealer I can still see some of the features of the lure through the paint, especially if I have patches of epoxy filler or adhesive from where I've installed rattles, weights or other items. Provided the sealer has been applied uniformly over the lure body this is not too much of a problem, but it would use a lot of sealer (and time) to keep going until the lure body is a uniform white. I don't bother to do this, preferring instead to move on and give the lure a coat or two of semi-opaque bright white. The sealer has already done its job and provided adhesion to the surface, but the semi-opaque white is far more effective at covering what's hidden beneath.

Suggested Settings For Sealer Coats:

- Reducing: 2 parts sealer to 3 parts reducer (filter after thinning).
- Air pressure: 30 PSI initially and adjust as required.

Coloring with Opaque Paints

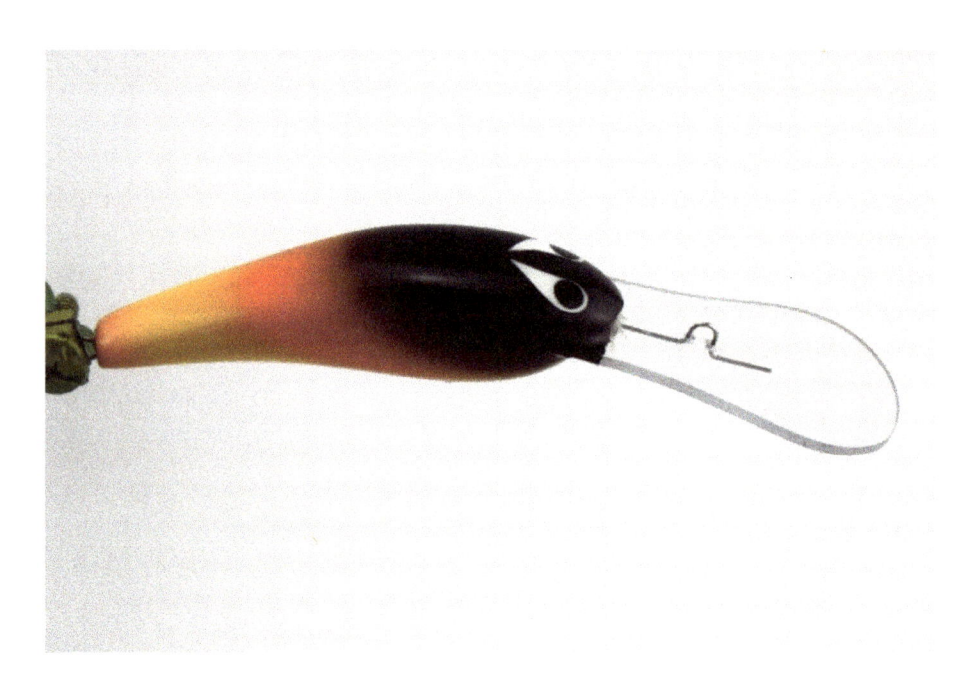

Opaque paints are perfect for anywhere you need solid colors. This lure was painted entirely using opaques.

Use opaque (aka semi-opaque) paints to:

- Paint an entire lure, or parts of a lure, one uniform color.
- Hide the features that are beneath the paint.
- Paint bold markings, bands or other features over base colors.

Basics Of Lure Painting

Opaque colors contain pigments that are made up from finely ground solid materials, which mean that they tend to obscure whatever is underneath. This is great if there are features that you want to hide (e.g. the edges of a foiled finish), or if you want a hard edge where there is a color change

Opaque paints can be used for shading, especially if they are thinned or lightened (more on this later), so you can get a good solid, even color on the back of your lure that fades away into the base colors as you move down the sides of the lure, for example.

Often I'll paint a lure pattern that is predominantly one particular color, with a plan to spray other opaque colors through masks or stencils later or maybe use a transparent paint to create graded color effects. Or both!

Suggested Settings For Opaque Paints:

- Reducing: 3 parts paint to 2 parts reducer (filter after thinning).
- Air pressure: 30-35 PSI initially and adjust as required.

Coloring/Shading Using Transparent Paints

This lure was painted yellow initially, and transparent cobalt blue was used to create a darker green back, shading to light green on the sides and yellow on the belly.

The photograph above is an example of using transparent paints to fade one color into the next. This entire lure was first sprayed bright opaque yellow. I then painted the back with several light coats of transparent blue paint, putting more coats on top and less down the sides so that the color changes gradually from bright green and slowly fades into the yellow base color. A splash of red on the throat and some dark bars on the side finish it off.

Use transparent paints to:

- Reveal features that you want to show through the paint, such as foil, transfers etc.
- Create new colors that are the combination of the base and transparent coats and blend or grade from one color to the next.
- Paint more subtle markings, bands or other features over base colors.
- Spray over metallic paints or aluminum base for a flashy, silvery color.

The color in transparent paints comes from liquid dyes rather than pigments, which means that they dry clear but colored and allow whatever features are underneath the paint to show through. When you spray transparent paint over a base color, the resulting effect is that you'll create a new color, the same as if you mixed the two paints. But the advantage of transparent paints is that you can shade by spraying the transparent more heavily in some areas and lighter in others. Transparent paints are also really useful for creating depth or for highlighting features. For example, a light spray of transparent paint to darken around the eye sockets of a lure can lift the eyes and make them really stand out.

Transparent paints are particularly useful for spraying over metallic/pearlescent paints and/or aluminum base. When you do this you'll find that you get a metallic version of the color. So for example, if you spray a lure metallic white and then overspray the back of the lure with transparent red you can get a lure that is metallic red on the back fading through various shades of pink to metallic white on the belly. Another example is spraying transparent cobalt blue over aluminum base, which creates a flashy, electric blue color that is brilliant for offshore lures. There are numerous other possibilities for this technique - I recommend experimenting and having fun with it!

Because transparent paints contain minimal solids to push through the nozzle of the airbrush, you'll find that you can use a little less reducer than you do for opaque paints, or you can use lower air pressure. I prefer to reduce the air pressure because keeping the paint thin gives me much better control over shading and so on.

Suggested Settings For Shading With Transparent Paints:

- Reducing: 3 parts paint to 2 parts reducer (filter after thinning).
- Air pressure: 30 PSI for general work, 20-25 PSI for more controlled shading.

Using Metallic And Pearlescent Paints

Metallic and pearlescent paints create a wonderful sheen and flash that fish often can't resist! Here a base color of metallic gold has been laid down.

Use metallic or pearlescent paints to:

- Add extra sparkle and flash to lure bodies.
- Better mimic the gold and silver sheens often observed on natural baitfish.
- Giving a lifelike sheen to sprayed scale patterns.

As the name suggests, metallic paints have very tiny particles of metal (aluminum) that are uniform in size and shape suspended in the paint matrix. When the paint is sprayed onto the lure, the orientation of these particles is random, causing them all to catch and reflect the light at different angles. Hence the sparkly effect that we are all familiar with. That sheen turns yellow into gold, gray into silver, orange into bronze and so on.

Pearlescent paints use the same principle, but instead of aluminum they use mica flake. Mica is a synthetic material that is similar in appearance to natural pearl but rather than reflect light it breaks it into its component wavelengths, creating a sheen that is slightly different to metallic paints.

If you really want to get technical, metallic paints maintain the same hue regardless of the angle you look at them, while pearlescent paints change hue depending on the angle of the light, so the lure appears to have lighted and shaded areas. At the end of the day, the two tend to be fairly interchangeable as far as we lure makers are concerned.

The main trick with metallic and pearlescent paints is not to spray any one coat too heavily - the same applies almost universally to airbrush paints but is particularly important with metallics and pearls. If the surface of the lure gets excessively wet, the suspended aluminum or mica flakes tend to clump together as the solvent dries, leaving you with a blotchy, spatter pattern appearance. This is made worse if your air pressure is relatively high or you have the nozzle of the airbrush too close to the lure body - the paint will be blown around as it dries and can be quite unsightly.

Aside from spraying light coats, there are four additional measures that I generally take when I'm airbrushing lures using metallic or pearlescent paints:

- The suspended flake makes these paints a little harder to push through a fine nozzle, so I often increase the air pressure to 35 or even 40 PSI.
- I'll often thin the paint a little more to make it flow better through a fine nozzle, although I generally don't do this if I'm using higher air pressures (it's one or the other).
- I hold the airbrush back a little further from the work piece to give some of the solvent a chance to dissipate and prevent the paint being blown about on the lure surface.
- I regularly mix the paint in the color pot by shaking and back flushing the paint. This stops the flake from settling in the bottom of the color cup.

There is another trick that works when you are using metallics and pearlescents with a dual action airbrush and are having trouble with the airbrush nozzle becoming clogged: reduce the air pressure. This might seem counter-intuitive because you'd expect higher pressure would push the stuff through. But using lower pressure allows you to pull the trigger back further without flooding the paint on. This in turn opens the throat of the airbrush more, providing a bigger opening at the nozzle for the particles to pass through.

Suggested Settings For Metallic And Pearlescent Paints:

- Reducing: 3 parts paint to 2 parts reducer (higher pressure) or 1:1 (lower pressure).
- Air pressure: 10-25 PSI for 1:1 reduced paint, 25-40 PSI for 3:2 reduced paint.

Fluorescent Paints

Fluorescent colors are great for dirty water and low light fishing. Here a fluorescent orange base coat is used.

Use fluorescent paints for:

- Bright, vibrant colors over a white base color.

Fluorescent paints are extremely popular in some quarters because of their ability to absorb light of a shorter wavelength and emit it as a longer one. This is what make the colors appear unnaturally bright. They are similar to opaque paints in terms of how they should be prepared and applied but are generally not useful for spraying over other paints because their ability to cover what lies beneath them is poor. It's certainly best to stick with a uniform bright white paint under fluorescent paints.

One thing to watch out for with fluorescent paints is that they are not UV stable, which means that they will fade over time.

Suggested Settings For Fluorescent Paints:

- Reducing: 3 parts paint to 2 parts reducer.
- Air pressure: 20-30 PSI.

Color Shift Paints

Use for:

- Fun and special effects!

Color shift paints are fun to play with and give great human appeal, even if the fish won't really notice! They contain microscopic flakes of aluminum coated with glass. The aluminum gives the paint sparkle and flash, while the glass splits white light into component wavelengths, which makes the paint look to be a different color depending on the angle of the light. Interestingly, color shift paints don't contain pigment themselves and are merely influencing the way the light behaves as it reflects, refracts and absorbs. They are designed to be sprayed over a base color, which then determines which wavelengths of the white light are reflected and which are absorbed.

Suggested Settings For Color Shift Paints:

- Reducing: 1:1 Paint to reducer.
- Air pressure: 20-30 PSI.

Blending, Tinting, Toning and Shading

Blending, tinting, toning and shading refer to the practice of modifying the color of your paint by mixing two or more colors together. To the beginner, this might seem unnecessary given the range of pre-mixed colors that are available from most airbrush paint manufacturers. However, you'll quickly find that you want to use colors that aren't in your collection or that you can't buy pre mixed. When that happens you have little option but to make them for yourself.

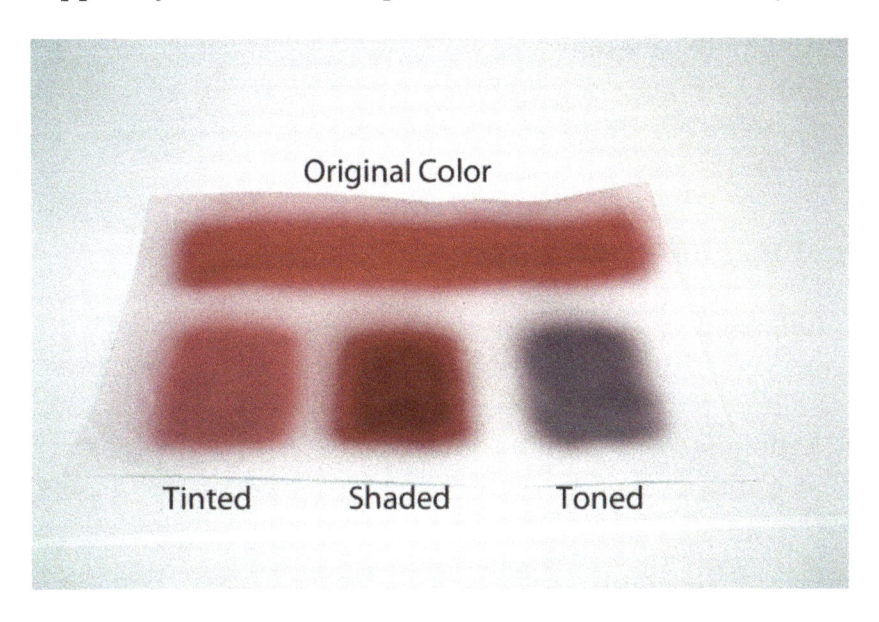

Test card showing the effect of tinting, shading and toning on AutoAir flame red.

We'll take a look at how you can use each of these processes in a minute, but first let's take a look at the terminology:

- **Mixing (or blending)** colors refers to creating a new color by mixing two different colors. For example, blue and green to make yellow, red and blue to

make purple and so on.
- **Tinting** refers to adding white to any color to lighten it.
- **Shading** refers to adding black to any color to darken it.
- **Toning** refers to adding both black and white to any color to reduce its brightness.
- **Coverage** refers to the ability to hide whatever color is underneath.

You can mix colors directly into the color pot on your airbrush, and I do this quite often. For example, if I was spraying a lure royal blue and wanted some darker blue spots around where the eyes were going to be, I'd wait until I'd finished with the base color, then add a drop (or less) of black paint to the color cup, give it a shake and go ahead and spray the darker spots.

Mixing directly into the color pot is fine for minor highlighting or shading. But if you need larger quantities of paint for a batch of lures, or if you are making lures to sell and want to be able to produce exactly the same color again next week, next month or even next year, then you need to do your mixing in a separate container and keep track of just exactly what ratios each color is mixed in. You need to record this in your very own recipe book!

Mixing and Blending Paint

If you've done some painting before, then you probably have a good idea of what two colors you might mix in order to create a particular third color, but if you are unsure then it's probably worth picking up an artist's color wheel from the local art supply store or online. They're cheap and they're an easy way to figure out what colors to mix and how to tint, tone or shade to get exactly what you are after.

If you've gone ahead and purchased the basic starter paint selection that I suggested earlier then you should have a bottle of each of the primary colors (red, yellow, and blue) plus black and white in both opaque and transparent. In theory, this should be everything you need to mix any color that you want - but in practice the primaries are generally not pure colors, so it's not a perfect strategy!

There are two ways you can achieve color blends: you can mix the paints together and then spray the mix, or you can spray one opaque color and then spray over the top with a transparent. Mixing the liquid paint is the way to go if you want the color to be the same shade wherever on the lure it is sprayed. Overspraying a base color with a transparent is more effective if you want two colors on your lure to fade smoothly from one into the other.

Opaque colors can generally be mixed with other opaque colors without any problems. They can also be mixed with transparent colors, although you'll find that the resulting paint has poorer coverage.

It is also possible to mix transparent colors with other transparent colors, which can be useful if you want to fade the newly created color into some other base color.

Blending is also useful when you are at the sealer stage – coloring up the sealer with a drop or two of the base color can save a little time later. I do this often when I'm making suspending jerkbaits and I want to keep the build up of paint to a minimum so as not to spoil the weight balance.

Tinting and Shading

Tinting is useful if you need a lighter shade of any color. As with mixing, it can be done in the color cup or by mixing the two colors before they go into the airbrush, or you can tint by overspraying your work with a transparent white paint.

Using a semi-opaque white paint for tinting increases coverage and creates a pastel color, while transparent white will tend to lighten and soften the color of opaque paint while reducing the coverage. Transparent white can also be used to tint other transparent colors.

Of course, the reverse is true with shading. Opaque paint can be darkened by adding either opaque black or transparent black into the color cup or mixing container, or you can shade by spraying transparent black over another color.

Shading adds depth to the color, although you have to be pretty careful to use the black sparingly as even very small amounts can easily overpower other colors.

Tone

Toning a color refers to tinting and shading at the same time, which might seem a little odd at first. But what it actually does is reduce the intensity of the color, makes it less vibrant and quite often brings it in line with colors observed in natural environments. In effect, toning can give lures a much more natural appearance to fish.

As with tinting and shading, toning can be done in the bottle or afterwards by spraying with transparent white, black or gray.

Aluminum Base

A lure that has been coated with aluminum base, ready for painting with transparent colors.

I'm sure some other brands offer this too, but AutoAir produces something that they refer to as "Aluminum Base", which comes in fine, medium and coarse, referring to the size of the aluminum particles suspended in the paint.

Basics Of Lure Painting

I love this product for the amazing flash that it produces and it is particularly good for saltwater lures. Aluminum base isn't intended to be left exposed, but rather to be painted over using a transparent color giving a finish that is much more reflective than a standard pearlescent or metallic paint. AutoAir recommends using an airbrush with a tip size of 0.5mm or larger for this product, but I've had little trouble shooting the fine base through my 0.3mm tip size Iwata HP CS airbrush. I just thin it a little more and drop the pressure down.

Like metallic and pearlescent paints, the flake in aluminum base has a tendency to pool and give the lure a dirty, blotchy appearance if you spray it too heavily. Sticking to light coats and drying thoroughly between coats will overcome this problem, but be aware that aluminum base can be slightly slower drying than most other airbrush paints.

Suggested Settings For Spraying Aluminum Base (fine):

- Reducing: 1:1 paint to reducer.
- Air pressure: 25 PSI initially and adjust as required.

Getting Started In Custom Painted Crankbaits

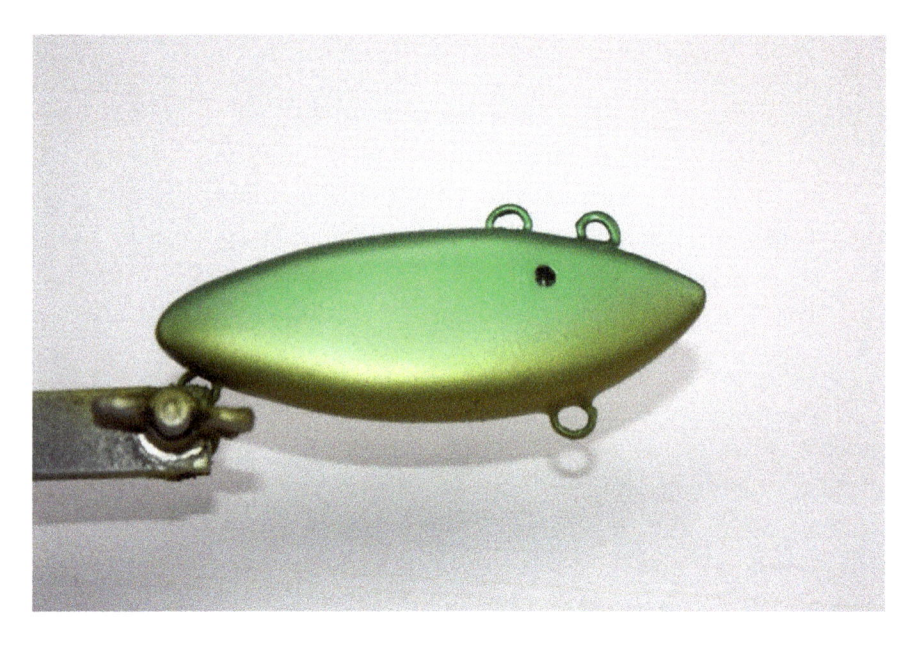

With transparent colors laid down over the aluminum base you get awesome sheen and flash – now it's time to add detail!

Lure Painting Techniques

So now we have the basics. We know how to prepare our lures, how to paint a base color and how to add shading, fade from one color to another and so on. Now the creative part begins! Now we can add details that will bring our lures to life using stencils, masks and other cool techniques.

Masking

Masking is the practice of using tape or some other self adhesive material to temporarily cover parts of your lure and shield them from paint as you spray other parts. It sounds simple enough, and it is, but there are a couple of pitfalls and a few things to know before you'll start getting perfect results.

Masking produces what we refer to as a 'hard edge'. In other words, there is a sharp line where the paint changes from whatever color you started with to the second color that you sprayed over the mask. This is desirable in some instances, but less desirable in others, depending on what you are trying to achieve. If you are a looking for a softer transition from one color to the next, then stencils are probably the better way to go, and we'll look at those next.

One of the down sides to masking is that it tends to be a one-off technique and is a little laborious. Usually a mask gets destroyed when you remove it from the lure and can't be reused, so you need to make one for each lure you intend to paint. Stencils, on the other hand, can be quickly and easily transferred to the next lure and reused.

Nonetheless, there are times when masking is the best (or the only) option, plus it's useful for protecting diving lips from paint, so there is still a place for this technique in my workshop.

Masking Materials

One of the first things that you'll need to know is what materials to use for masking. Choose the right ones and things will go smoothly, choose the wrong ones and you're going to enjoy your airbrushing a whole bunch less!

If you are planning to use tape for masking off parts of your lures then you need to find one with the following properties:

- It must be low tack, or you risk tearing off the base color when you remove the tape.
- It must be non-textured. Most masking tapes have a slight wrinkle to the surface, which is fine if you're painting the walls of your house, but if you're after fine detail on a lure it allows paint to bleed under the edge.
- It must leave no residual stickiness on the lure surface. PVC duct tape is a good example - it is low enough tack and non-textured, so it gives a great, sharp edge to your paint, but it often leaves a residue that spoils the paint underneath the tape.

Not surprisingly, the best tapes are the ones that are made for the automotive painting industry, such as the Scotch Blue and plastic striping tape.

Another great (although slightly more expensive) option is artists frisket film, which is a clear or matt plastic, low tack self adhesive masking material that works quite well for lure making.

And a final product that I sometimes use for masking parts of my lures is liquid frisket, which is a latex based fluid that can be brushed on to parts of the lure that you want shielded from the paint. Liquid frisket is removed after painting simply by rubbing your thumb gently over the mask and rolling it off. I don't use liquid frisket a lot, but I do find it useful for masking around the mouth of surface poppers to give a clean edge from the red mouth to the body color, and I also sometimes use it for masking the diving lip of crankbaits before spraying, or for creating spots and dots for frog patterns and so on.

Lure Painting Techniques

Applying a Mask

Tape and frisket masks can be applied in one of two ways: You can either cut the desired shapes before the mask is applied and then transfer it to the lure body, or you can put the tape or film on the lure body first and then cut out the areas that you want the paint to reach.

Clear frisket film is awesome for masking. It allows me to see what's under the mask and gives crisp, clean edges.

If I'm working with paper tape and I want to the pattern I'm spraying to be a mirror image on both sides of the lure I usually cut the pattern first and then place the tape onto the lure body. One way that I do this is to apply a piece of tape to an overhead transparency film, then turn the film over and apply a piece of tape to the other side. Then I hand-draw my pattern onto the tape and cut it out using a sharp scalpel. With care, the tape can be removed from each side of the plastic sheet and transferred to the lure for a perfect mirror image. The plastic sheet just stops the two pieces of tape from becoming inseparable.

One of the great advantages of frisket film is that it is transparent, which makes it really easy to get mirror images on. I often print an image of the pattern I'm after onto a piece of white paper, place it under the frisket and trace the outline onto the film using a very fine pointed felt tipped pen. Then I apply the frisket to the lure and cut the shape out using a scalpel.

When getting a perfect mirror image on each side of the lure isn't important I might simply cover the lure with tape, draw my desired pattern onto it and then cut it out while the tape remains stuck to the lure. Obviously, I use only very light pressure on the scalpel, so only the tape gets cut and I don't cut into the paint beneath.

Tips for Spraying Through a Mask

The finished lure after the frisket tape mask has been peeled off.

- Ensure that the tape or frisket is properly bedded down. Use a smooth, hard object to gently work along the edges of the mask and ensure that it is in full contact with the lure. Remove wrinkles or areas where the paint might get underneath.
- Reduce your airbrush pressure to as low as you can while still getting good atomisation of the paint. Lower pressures reduce the risk of paint being forced under the tape. I routinely work at around 15 PSI when I'm spraying through a mask, but it depends what I'm spraying and how thin the paint is.
- Hold the airbrush a little further back than you would normally, again to

reduce the risk of paint being forced under the mask.
- The first couple of coats should be very lightly dusted on and should be heat set before the next coat is applied. This will form a seal along the edge of the mask and prevent subsequent coats from penetrating underneath.
- Avoid getting the surface visibly wet, especially for the first few coats.
- Transparent base can be your friend when you are masking. A couple of coats of this will seal the edge of the mask and preserve clean lines. Then you simply paint over it with your top color.
- Remove the mask very gently by pulling parallel with the surface of the lure so that the tape is basically rolling back over itself. Never pull the tape off vertically (i.e. at right angles), or you risk lifting the top color and/or the base color.

Stencilling

With a little practice (and a quality airbrush) some quite complex effects can be achieved using simple stencils.

Technically, stencils are the female versions of masks, but in lure making a stencil is usually assumed to be something held in front of the lure rather than stuck physically on it. Stencils can be held in one hand while you spray with the other, or they can be held using tape, clamps or some kind of jig.

Stencilling doesn't always give the same sharp, clean edge between paint colors as masking does, although you can get pretty close with a little care. The main advantages of stencils over masks are:

- Once you've made them or have a collection from which to choose, stencils are faster to use than masks. You usually need only make them once and then you can re-use them.
- By resting a stencil on the lure you can get a reasonably sharp edge to your painting, but the same stencil can be used to get a softer, more blurry effect simply by holding it up and away from the lure body. The greater the distance between the stencil and the lure, the softer and more blurry the line becomes.
- You don't need a mirror image: spray one side of the lure, give the stencil a wipe, turn it over and spray the other side. Voilà! You have the same pattern on each side.

Stencils can be made from all kinds of household items including paper, thin card, plastic film, PET bottles and so on. However, my favorite material is the Mylar stencil film that is made specifically for this task. I like this material because it's easy and convenient to use, but mostly because it's solvent proof. At the end of a day's painting I can drop my stencils into a tub of denatured alcohol (methylated spirit) and leave them to soak overnight. By morning they just need a wipe with some tissue or paper towel and they're as good as new.

Sometimes I'll draw my desired pattern onto the stencil film by hand with a very fine tipped sharpie. Other times I will print it onto a piece of paper, tape the paper to the stencil film and trace the outline with a sharpie. Stencil film is semi transparent, so you can clearly see your lure design underneath. Once the design is transferred to the film I either cut it out using a scalpel, or I use a stencil cutter.

To use stencils effectively you need some way to hold your lure securely so that you can keep one hand free to control the airbrush and the other one to place the stencil where you need it. I make my own lure holding clamps, which I'll show you later, but you can also use helping hands if you prefer.

Stencils From Household Items

Stencils don't have to be made from the latest high tech, laser cut materials. I've used all kinds of household items as stencils at various times, including:

- Hair combs for painting vertical stripes and bars.
- Ring binder reinforcers for making eyes and spots.
- Wire and plastic mesh for scales.
- Old paint brushes with some bristles cut out for ragged edge stripes.
- Bathroom fan cover for curved vertical bars.

Keep an eye open for everyday items that can be used as stencils or masks for your lure painting. Ordinary photocopier paper and hair combs are good examples.

Keep your eyes open as you go about your day to day activities and with a little imagination you'll find that there are all kinds of items that can be used as stencils!

Tips For Using Stencils

- Reduce your air pressure. Most stencil films, paper and thin card are soft and flexible, so blasting them with compressed air will make them flap around. I often work at around 20 PSI when I'm spraying stencils, but it varies depending on the paint dilution, type of paint and what I'm trying to achieve.
- Have an extra hand. You need to hold your lure, airbrush and the stencil all at once and most of us only have two hands...... find a way to hold your lure so your hands are free for the airbrush and stencil!
- Light coats are the order of the day. The nice thing about stencils is that you can usually take them away to see how your work is progressing and with a little care you can place them back where they were to spray extra coats.

- Light coats and low air pressure will reduce overspray and bounce back, giving you a better result.
- Keep your airbrush perpendicular to the lure at all times. In other words, you need to lock your wrist and move the airbrush back and forth in a way that the paint is directed straight at the stencil. If you bend your wrist you will direct paint under the stencil and spoil your work.

Spraying Crayfish Shells And Fish Gills

I use very simple stencils for spraying these features on my lures, often just a paper stencil cut with a pair of scissors or a scalpel. For these features to have a 3-D appearance, you want to create a hard edge on one side with the paint fading away into the background color on the other side.

I find that the best way to get this effect is by holding the stencil flat on the work and spraying the stencil, not the lure. Imagine that you are trying to spray a line along the inside edge of the stencil. If you focus on doing this, the overspray will go onto the lure and give you the effect that you're after. I find that it's best to thin the paint well with reducer and work at around 5-10 PSI, which gives a lot of control over the paint delivery. Be sure to build the color up with a couple of light coats to avoid ugly paint runs.

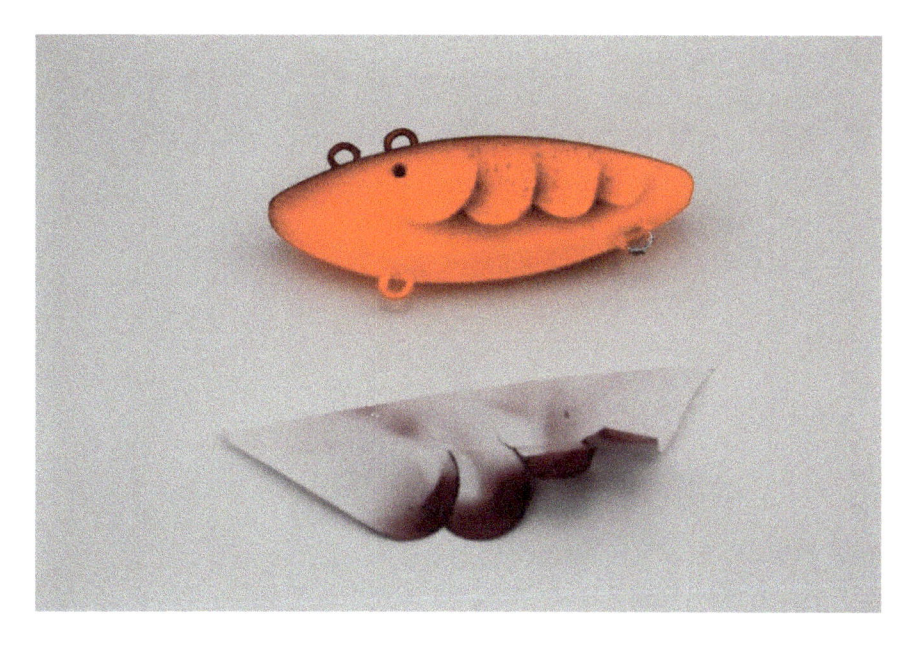

Simple paper masks and stencils can be used to impart amazing depth to a design.

Tips For Painting Speckle, Spots and Spatter

There are times when you'll want to create spots, dots, blotches, spatter and so on. Sometimes these spots might be fairly large, such as when you're painting the distinctive spots on the side of a sardine pattern or a brown trout imitation. Other times you might need a fine mist of "freckles", such as the dots on the back of a rainbow trout imitation. Likewise, these spots can be hard-edged, or softer edged, depending on your needs.

Here are some tips for painting spots and dots:
- Freehand dots are possible if you have a dual action airbrush (single actions ones can be used but tend to spatter). Freehand dots tend to be round and soft edged.
- For larger sized, hard-edged round dots you can use paper punches to make holes in frisket or tape. Just stick the tape where you want the dot, spray through the hole and then remove the tape

Getting Started In Custom Painted Crankbaits

- Hard edged dots can also be painted using the blunt end of drill bits, simply by dipping them in paint and dabbing it onto the lure.
- Random, spatter effects can be achieved by dipping small artists brushes into some paint and then, holding the brush over your lure, rubbing your thumb over the bristles, causing them to flick.

Speckling, spots and spatter are common features of many lures.

- A technique I sometimes use when I'm painting frog patterns is the "blue tac" mask. I paint the lure body the color that I want the spots to be, then simply stick small pieces of blue tac anywhere I want a spot. Then I spray my main body color and I rub off the blue tac with my thumb....wha-la! The result is random sized and shaped spots with softish edges.
- Liquid frisket can be useful for painting sharp edged spots. It's used much the same way as blue tac – except it's painted on or dotted with toothpicks, nails, drill bits or whatever you like!

There are a couple of airbrush techniques that can be used when you want a smattering of finer spots. Here's how they work:

- The first technique works with any dual action airbrush, but requires a bit of practice to get it right. With the air not flowing, hold your airbrush with the needle pointing downwards and pull back on the trigger a few times (don't press it, we want paint flow but not air flow at this stage). Point the airbrush at the lure and just tap on the trigger a couple of times to create a quick burst of air with no paint flow. What this does is load the tip of the needle up with some paint and then blast it off with a little burst of air, causing speckles and dots.
- The second technique is my favorite, but it only works with a couple of the Iwata airbrushes that I'm aware of, the HP-CP I use is one - other brands don't seem to have this ability. Remove both the needle cap and the nozzle cap from the airbrush....... that's it! Now when you spray you'll get a very nice spatter effect. Reduce the air pressure for bigger spots, increase it for a more uniform covering of small spots! Be careful not to damage the airbrush needle while you're doing this!

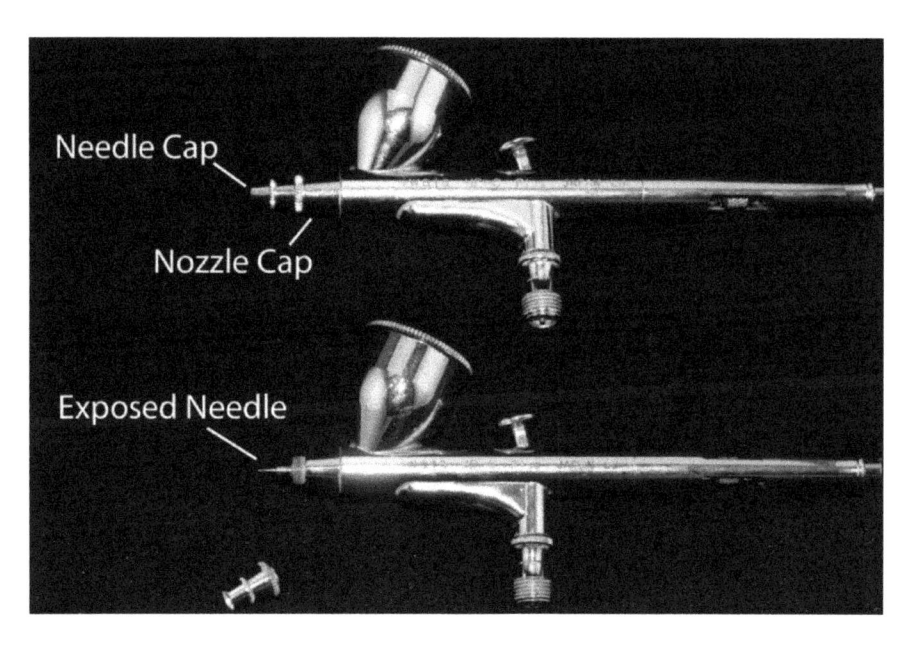

Removing both the needle cap and the nozzle cap from the Iwata HP-CP airbrush turns it into a handy tool for painting speckles.

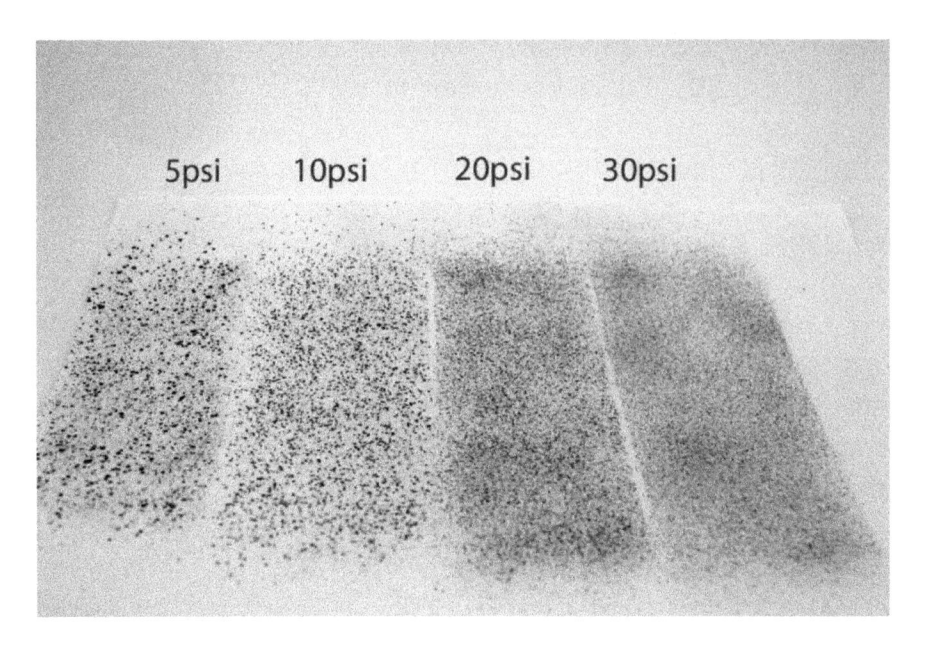

A test card showing the effect of adjusting air pressure when using the HP-CP airbrush without the nozzle cap. Low pressure (left) creates larger spots, higher pressure (right) creates a more uniform mist of finer speckles.

Getting a Scale Effect

Painting scale patterns on your lures is basically just another stencilling technique, but because it's something that lure makers do quite a lot of I'm going to address this separately.

There are lots of different ways that you can go about spraying scale, but of course the first thing that you're going to need is some material to use as a stencil. Fortunately, there are numerous sources:

- Tulle fabric from the haberdashery shop can be purchased for a few dollars a length and will last a lifetime of lure painting.
- A loofah from the supermarket contains a lot of scale stencil - just cut the string that holds it all together and you're in business (don't recycle an old

one from the bathroom, you don't want soap scums, body oils and the like anywhere near your lures).
- Any kind of fabric or plastic mesh can potentially be used - my collection of meshes includes onion bags, water filter covers, metallic ribbon, mosquito netting and decorative products from craft and office supply shops, among others.

Spraying through soft mesh is a simple way to create scale effects, although purpose designed stencils can also be purchased.

All of these sources will give you scale patterns that are essentially hexagonal, but you can also get purpose-made, laser-cut scale stencils from specialist airbrush suppliers, such as lurelayouts.com.

There are lots of different ways that you can hold your scaling stencil over the lure body while you paint. A lot of folks stretch the scaling material inside a small embroidery hoop, and then lay it against the lure while they spray through it.

My preferred approach is to simply wrap the netting around the lure and hold it in place with a handful of bulldog and/or alligator clips, as shown in the picture below. The reason I like this is that you can change colors, put the lure down and come back to it and so on and the mesh stays in place.

You need to pay a little attention to make sure that the scales are properly aligned on the lure body and that the mesh is sitting flat on the surface anywhere that you want the scales to be clear and sharp. The following routine works pretty well for me.

Using transparent paints to create scales gives a subtle result.

Tips For Spraying Scales

- Reduce air pressure and spray light coats. Most of the mesh fabrics that are used for painting scale effects are very fine and it's easy to blow paint underneath and spoil the effect if your air pressure is too high, have the nozzle too close to your work or if you put the paint on too heavily.
- Keep your wrist locked so that the airbrush remains perpendicular to the lure surface at all times. Move your whole arm back and forth as you spray.
- With an embroidery hoop it's usually not easy to remove and replace scale

fabric accurately, you really only get one shot at it.

Painting a dark color over a light base color will give you dark scales with a light margin. Light colors can also be sprayed over dark ones, although it may take more coats to get the coverage you require.

- A good way to get a subtle scale effect is to paint the lure in the desired color and then spray through the scale mesh using the same color that has been lightly shaded by adding a small amount of transparent black.
- Another good but subtle way to paint scale is to lightly dust the mesh with metallic gold, silver or bronze, just enough to give the lure a little glaze of color.

Using Transparent Base

I use transparent base for a couple of important things: inter-coating and paint cover reduction.

Intercoating

Intercoating is the process of spraying a clear coat over your painted lure before you spray another coat or apply the clear finish. I don't intercoat all that often, but it can be quite useful if you find that your lure has been left with a textured surface as a result of paint build up around scale mesh, masks or heavy metallic flake. A few coats of transparent base can help build the finish and smooth out these lumps and bumps. This isn't too much of a problem when you are finishing your lures with Devcon 2K or Etex because they both build a thick coat of clear that smooths over minor surface inconsistencies.

Paint Cover Reduction

Most of us have experienced the frustration of paints that have poor coverage - it means that we have to paint a lot of coats in order to cover whatever is underneath. Transparent base can be used to reduce the coverage even further!

Why would we want to do that?

I find it's particularly useful when I am shading with transparent black paint and want really controlled paint delivery so that I can build the color slowly. It's also handy if I want to get a fine smattering of metallic over a base color and want to build up gradually until I am happy with the result. It's very easy to accidentally overdo it and overpower the base color when you are doing this.

Reducing the paint is an option, but I find that sometimes I have to over-reduce it in order to dilute the color to the desired extent. Then you're spraying super thin paint, which has its own drawbacks.

Instead, I might mix transparent black paint and transparent base 1:1 or even 1:2. Then I reduce the mixture 3:2 with reducer, just as I would any other transparent paint. This maintains the body of the paint so it's not too thin, but reduces the intensity of the color, giving me a lot of control over the shading process. The same thing can be done with other colors, for example if you were painting transparent blue over opaque red to get purple, you could do the same thing - mixing your blue 1:1 with transparent base before reducing will give you a lot of control to build the shading very gradually.

Foiled Finishes

One of the drawbacks of waterborne and water based paints is that the technology to create chrome effects doesn't currently exist. Foil is kind of like the "poor man's chrome" and is an alternative way to increase the reflectiveness of your lure. It isn't quite in the same class as a mirror-like chrome finish, but it certainly gives a good amount of flash and can look great.

The Kitchen Foil Finish

The great thing about foiling is that it doesn't require any fancy equipment or materials - just plain old kitchen foil and some Etex will do a fine job for a basic foil finish.

Lure Painting Techniques

Everyday kitchen foil can be used to great effect. Rubbing it on a textured surface can give a sense of depth to the finished lure.

I'm going to talk you through my process for making a basic foiled finish, but you can also make textured foil finishes like the one shown in the picture below. This is one of the project lures and project finishes that my Crankbait Masterclass participants learn, and it's only slightly more involved than a basic foil finish.

One of the problems with foiled finishes is that you can't use the airbrush sealer because you don't want to obscure the foil beneath. In fact, this is about the only time when I paint lures without using sealer! Well, not entirely true - I do seal beneath the foil!

Here is my basic process:

- Prepare and seal the lure in the normal way. I prefer to use Etex with titanium dioxide mixed in, which gives me a nice surface to work on.
- Cut your foil to the desired size and shape using a sharp scalpel or a pair of scissors.
- Give your lure a generous coat of Etex (without the titanium dioxide, this

Getting Started In Custom Painted Crankbaits

time). Then carefully lay your foil on the lure body and smooth out the wrinkles. I wear a pair of disposable gloves for this and simply move the foil to where I want it using my fingers.

- Bed the foil down and make sure it is completely flat on the lure surface. Because of the curvature of the lure it is unavoidable that there will be some minor wrinkles and creases, just get it as good as you can and accept it can't be perfect!
- Now gently brush Etex all over the lure, being careful not to move the foil during the process. Once you have the entire lure coated, your foil is effectively encased, with Etex above and below.
- Put your lures onto a rotating drying rack and leave them for at least 24 hours to cure. Then wet sand the Etex with 400 grit paper to remove the The color coats can now be applied in the normal fashion. This is the one time when I don't use a sealer – transparent paint over foil can look fantastic! I often use opaque white to spray over the edges of the foil so that they blend in with the background and aren't obvious.

A flat sided crankbait finished with foil to create a skeleton effect. In this case, kitchen foil was textured using gang nails, but you can use whatever is available to you.

Lure Painting Techniques

The Foil Tape Approach

Foil tape is an easy way to create flash and metallic effects when over-sprayed with transparent paints.

Aluminum foil tape is readily available at many hardware stores and on EBay, Amazon etc. I personally prefer the kitchen foil technique because I believe the results I get that way are better and stronger. With foil tape you are relying on the tape not delaminating from the lure body, which I've heard can sometimes happen but have never personally experienced. Nonetheless, many lure makers swear by the stuff, so I guess it comes down to personal experiences and preferences. It certainly makes foiling easy to do!

Here's the basic process:

- Cut a piece of foil tape to the size and shape you need. Texture it by placing it on a texture surface (shiny side down) and gently rubbing your thumb over the tape.
- Remove the backing and place the foil where you need it to be, then smooth it down, being careful not to flatten any design you have rubbed into it.
- Give the entire lure a coat of Etex and place it on a rotating drying wheel so the Etex can level out and cure.

Getting Started In Custom Painted Crankbaits

That's it! Of course, you'll want to wet sand the Etex with 400 grit paper to remove the gloss and then you're ready to paint.

A lipless crankbait finished using foil tape, which was then coated with clear epoxy before spraying with transparent colors.

Water-Slide Transfers

If you're looking for an easy way to get that fine detail, then water slide transfers are just the ticket!

It's outside of the scope of this book to cover in detail how this is done, but I'll give a brief overview. Basically, what you need to do is create a design on a computer and then print it onto special water slide transfer paper. Then carefully cut the design out using a scalpel and cutting mat.

Lure Painting Techniques

Using a laser printer to create water slide decals is a neat way to add some detail to your lures.

When this paper is placed in water the backing sheet comes off and the printed material can be slid onto your lure. If you've ever made model aircraft or trains, you'll be familiar with these transfers. Once the transfer dries, it becomes permanent and can be painted over using transparent colors or simply clear coated.

Slide transfer paper comes in white and clear, which one you use will depend on what you're doing.

The paper also comes in laser and inkjet versions. The inkjet paper must be sprayed with several coats of acrylic clear after printing, or the ink will run when it gets wet. My experience has been that because of this extra step, the inkjet paper doesn't conform as easily to the contours of the lure and generally gives an inferior result. If you don't have access to a color laser printer it's still worth buying the laser paper and paying a couple of bucks to get it printed.

Putting Eyes On Lures

Many anglers think that eyes are the most important part of decorating lures. I'm not sure what it is about an eye that attracts the strikes, but they do. And as always there are a few options for creating them.

Hand Painted Eyes

I often hand-paint eyes onto my lures. I use bright red, white or yellow paint, which I apply by dipping the blunt end of a drill bit into paint, then dabbing it onto the lure. Once this is dry I repeat the process using a smaller drill bit and some black paint. With a little practice you can do quite a neat job using this technique. I like drill bits for this because I can buy a cheap set for $5 and have a range of sizes for the iris and pupils. Lots of folks use nails or dowels for this, which works fine too.

Dabbing eyes onto a lure using a drill bit and some paint takes a little practice, but it gives your lures a nice, crisp traditional look.

Hand-painting eyes on lures can be a very frustrating pastime, and getting it right can take considerable practice. These are my best tips for getting it right:
- Don't start by painting eyes directly onto your best, hard earned lures. Practice first on pieces of scrap wood or electrical conduit and move on to

lures when you are having some success.
- I like to paint the eyes before I put the final clear coat on, so they get a protective coating over them.
- A good strategy if you plan to apply more than one coat of clear finish is to paint the eyes after the first coat of clear but before the second coat goes on. By doing this you can wipe the eyes off using a paper towel dampened with alcohol and not have to worry about removing the rest of your paint job. This allows you to paint and repaint the eyes until you are 100% happy with them, then put another coat of clear over the top to finish them off.

Adhesive Eyes

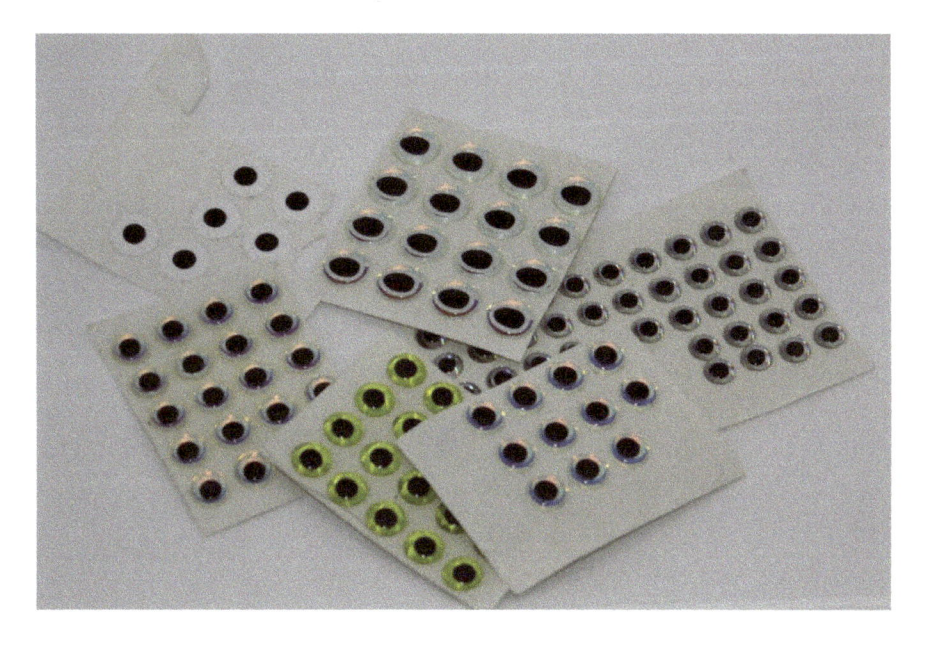

Self adhesive plain, holographic and 3D eyes can be purchased online and make getting a professional finish very easy.

An easy approach to putting eyes on your lures is to use the self adhesive varieties that are available online in plain, holographic or 3D.

I used to consider using adhesive eyes to be cheating, but these days I'm often happy to use them because they give me professional results very quickly. There really isn't much to tell you about using the plain and holographic types;

just take them off the backing paper and stick them straight onto the lure, then clear coat over them.

I use several types of 3D eyes. One type I purchase from a supplier is a solid resin eye with an adhesive backing. The eyes come in a range of colors, always with a black pupil. These can be used in exactly the same way as the paper or holographic adhesive eyes I have described above, but I often drill a shallow hole to recess this style of eye rather than just sticking it to the lure surface. This protects it from being knocked off during fishing and gives a very pleasing appearance.

Other times I will stick the 3D eye to the lure without recessing it and will simply ensure that it gets several coats of clear to firmly bond it to the lure. This approach is great if you want to create very bold, obvious eyes.

3D eyes that have been stuck directly to the surface of the lure (left) and recessed by drilling a suitable hole first (right).

Airbrushed Eyes

Airbrushing eyes onto your lures can create a pleasing result. Simple paper stencils or frisket masks work fine and you can get some great effects.

I'm sure there are plenty of artists around who are so skilled with an airbrush that they can paint eyes brilliantly using freehand techniques. I'm not one of them!

I make stencils for airbrushing eyes from frisket and the removable self adhesive dots you can buy at office supply stores. For making frisket masks I simply cut a couple of squares of frisket and then punch holes in them using hollow punches. A larger hole is used for the eye and a smaller one for the pupil.

As always, I leave painting the eyes until last, and I give the entire lure a clear coat before I start painting the eyes, in case I need to remove them and start over.

The great thing about airbrushing eyes is the flexibility you have with colors. You can get some really great effects by painting the eye first with a light colored metallic paint or a pearlescent color. Then you can use either an opaque or transparent color to paint the pupil, maybe even with a tiny glint of white to give the appearance of a sparkle in the eye.

The other great thing about airbrushing eyes is that you can spend some time getting the stencils in the right place and can remove and replace them as you need to in order to get the eye and pupil exactly as you want it. Once you have the stencil in place you can very quickly add the finishing touches.

Clear Coating and Finishing

A clear finish coat will protect the paint and give your lure a professional, glossy look. There are many clear coating products, including marine epoxy, polyurethane and polyamide. All of these have their pros and cons and as usual you will need to experiment and find what works for you with the paints you're using.

One sound piece of advice that I can offer when it comes to the clear coating is *not to rush the process.* I mentioned earlier that paint incompatibilities can result in major problems and these are almost always due to solvents reacting with each other. The longer you leave a lure after each painting step, the more solvent can dissipate and the less likely there will be compatibility problems.

Etex (Envirotex Lite)

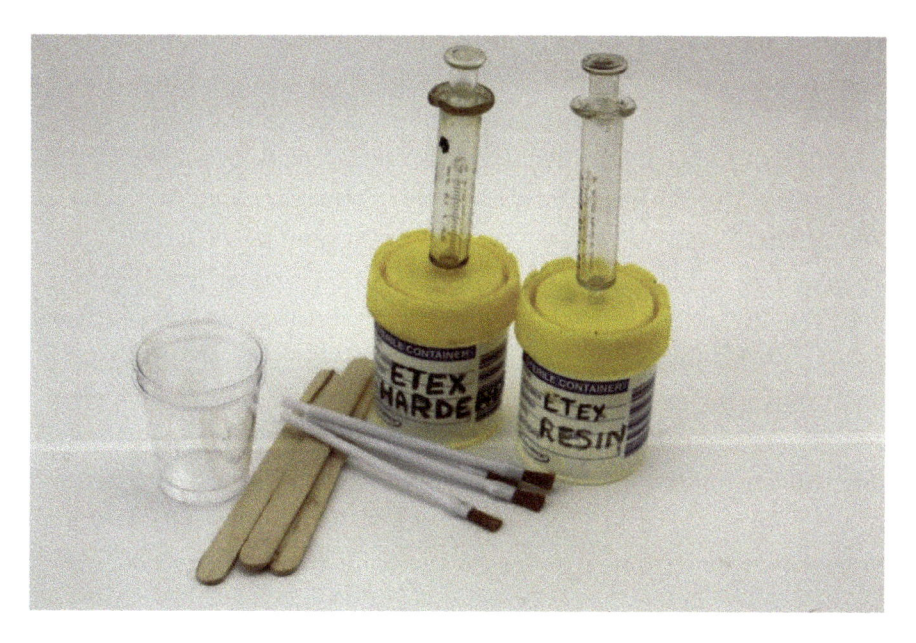

This is my setup for dispensing small amounts of Etex. All-glass syringes are best, as rubber seals perish and contaminate the resin. The containers are medical specimen jars from the pharmacy with holes drilled in the top.

Getting Started In Custom Painted Crankbaits

'Envirotex Lite' (Etex) is one of my favorite clear coats for lure making. It is super tough, crystal clear and gives a deep, wet look that I haven't seen matched by any other product.

Etex can be pretty temperamental to work with at times, but here is what generally works for me:

- I warm my Etex by putting the bottles under a heat lamp, halogen light or other warm spot. Don't overdo this, making it too hot will drastically reduce your working time, increase toxic fumes and give your lures a poor finish. You just need to gently warm it to make the liquid more runny, which reduces bubbles and helps it flow on better.
- I mix my Etex in disposable plastic shot glasses using a flat stick. I know some folks reckon a round mixing stick reduces bubbles, but I haven't found this to be the case.
- After mixing I put the shot glass in a warm place and leave it for 5 minutes or so to let some of the bubbles dissipate.
- Then I use a disposable brush to put the finish on to the lure, brushing back and forth over the lure to ensure that it gets worked well into the surface.
- Next I use a gas barbecue match to create carbon dioxide that causes the small surface bubbles that have formed to dissipate. I find I get best results if I hold the flame above the lure and move it briskly across the surface just barely touching the finish. This quickly pops bubbles without overheating and burning the Etex.
- I usually put the lure onto a rotating drying rack to prevent the Etex from running to the lowest point, but occasionally I'll simply hang it to dry.
- About every 15 minutes for the first 60-90 minutes I go back to the lures and check that the Etex is still even and that there are no dry patches. If there are dry patches I brush over them with the disposable brush. Bubbles or dust in the finish are usually best removed using a sharp pin.
- All that is left to do at this stage is to put a cover over the lures to keep any dust away and leave them in a warm place for 48 hours or so while the resin cures.

Take the normal chemical handling precautions whenever you are working with Etex - gloves are essential, as is eye protection. Be sure to read and follow the instructions on the bottle. The latest Etex formula doesn't contain solvents and is a lot less smelly than earlier versions of the product, but that doesn't mean that the vapours are harmless. Be sure to work in a well ventilated place and/or wear a suitable mask for personal protection.

Note: It is possible to spray Etex onto your lures, but it requires significant thinning to get it flowing through a spray gun or airbrush. The advantages are that the finish doesn't tend to get bubbles or dust when it's sprayed on thin. The disadvantage is that it takes a couple of coats to build up a thick finish, and you need a dedicated airbrush or spray gun as the stuff is difficult to remove once it starts to cure. Personal protection is critical when spraying this finish.....In short I would **not** recommend it to recreational lure makers, especially beginners.

Devcon 2-Ton

A lot of lure makers use the two part epoxy "Devcon 2-Ton", which is actually an adhesive but is reasonably clear and glossy and makes quite a good finish. The set time is around 30 minutes, and like Etex it is relatively thick and must be brushed onto the lures with a disposable brush.

Devcon is slightly less clear than Etex, but tends to be a lot easier to apply and is a fair bit faster drying, which results in less opportunity for dust to get onto the surface and spoil it.

I don't use Devcon a lot because I personally prefer the finish I get with Etex. I've also noticed that Etex seems to be a little more elastic that Devcon, so it's less prone to developing fine cracks around the hook hangers and tow points.

Moisture Cure Urethane (MCU)

While Etex and Devcon both create beautiful and very durable clear finishes, they are messy and fiddly to apply and are a real headache when things go pear-shaped.

Two pack polyurethane clear coats are used extensively in the automotive industry and when applied to lures they result in a clear coat that is hard and glossy. It's not quite to the same standard as Etex or Devcon, but it's still tougher, better looking and more durable than the paint on many commercial lures.

There is just one problem: They are highly toxic. In fact, in most countries they can only legally be sprayed in a registered spray booth whilst wearing a full body suit, tight fitting goggles, gloves and respirator. It's not something I'd recommend to recreational lure makers!

But fortunately there is an alternative.

Moisture cure polyurethanes (MCU) are a different formulation and are single part clear coats for which the curing process is accelerated by nothing more than moisture in the atmosphere. The finish isn't quite as tough as the two part polyurethanes, but it's still pretty durable and is a much easier and more convenient way to finish lures that Etex or Devcon.

These chemicals are still very toxic, so don't be tempted to spray them onto your lures, but they actually work quite well for dipping lures. Because there are no airborne droplets, if you wear gloves and a respirator, work in a well ventilated place and don't leave the lid off the tin for a minute longer than you need to, you can keep health risks reasonably low. As always, follow the manufacturer's instructions and follow health and safety guidelines for these products.

The mainstream use for MCU is for putting a super tough, clear and glossy finish on hardwood floors, so as you'd imagine there are quite a few brands of MCU on the market. It can be confusing as to which one is the best for lure making, so here is the big tip: you don't want either a water based or oil modified polyurethane....you want moisture cured!

Dick Nite S81, Garco and Famowood are all good MCU products that you can use for clear coating lures, but you'll find equivalent products at most paint and hardware stores. They all vary slightly in their characteristics so as always, trial and error is the only option. Always read the manufacturer's instructions when using these products.

Unlike epoxy and Etex, the solvents in MCU tend to react with solvent based paints, so if you are using aerosols you'll need to test whether it will be compatible with whatever you are using and once again, be prepared to wait until the paint is absolutely dry and there are no residual solvent vapours. If you can get even a hint of a smell, put the lure aside until the smell is completely gone.

If you are using acrylic paints and are planning to use MCU to clear coat it is best to seal the wood with epoxy and titanium dioxide, rather than wood hardener. I would also recommend not using the oil based primer/sealer/undercoat, instead just painting with a white water-based sealer and then with your color coats.

One of the problems that occurs with MCU is the lifting or bubbling of paint under the clear coat, and often this seems to have something to do with solvent in the MCU getting trapped as the outside of the coating starts to gel and go hard. This problem is worse if you put the lures on a rotating drying rack, because it keeps the excess MCU on the lure. Hanging the lures so the excess MCU can run to the tail and be removed by occasional blotting seems to solve the problem most of the time and is a pretty simple solution!

Note: It takes very little moisture to cause MCU to start curing, and when it does your entire tin of paint will start to gel. To avoid this you need to work in a dry environment and keep exposure to air and water to an absolute minimum. Decanting a small amount of MCU into a wide mouth jar that you can dip your lures into helps minimise the number of times you open the tin. Spraying a product like bloxygen or some bottled CO_2 into your storage containers can also help keep the clear coat useable for much longer.

Other Clear Coating Options

An entire book could be written just on the subject of clear coating alone. There are so many products that could be used, everyone has their favorites and we all have different needs when it comes to the end result.

Those I've covered so far are the ones that I personally keep coming back to because I feel they give superior results with minimal fuss. There may be better options out there (and I'll keep looking for them), but over decades of lure making, these have been the stand-outs for me.

I've tried dozens of other products over the years too. And I get asked so many times by so many people about their own favorite clear coats that I decided to at least mention a few here. With all of these products you will need to test how they react with the paint system you have used. Solvents used in some of these can react with airbrush acrylics, causing them to "fry up", craze, wrinkle or run. Try any new product on a lure that you don't really care about first!

Iso-free 2 Packs

There are a few isocyanate free two pack clear coats available these days, and although I don't have personal experience with many of them, I understand that they generally play nicely with airbrush acrylics. Most of these are epoxy or enamel products and they dry very clear and very hard. If you use these with an airbrush you'll find that they are a pain to clean up, especially if they start to gel. Before you contemplate using iso-free clears please study the material safety data sheets carefully. Iso-free does not mean non toxic, and most of them contain a cocktail of highly toxic, cancer causing chemicals, along with highly flammable solvents. Masks, gloves, suits and proper spray booths are required to use these safely.

Two Pack Urethanes

A commonly used product in lure making circles is polyurethane clear coat used for timber floors. It's hard, can be dipped (i.e. a little less hazardous to the lungs) and reasonably clear. The main reason I shy away from these is that most of them don't have the clarity of Etex.

Two pack automotive clears also fall into this category. They certainly have clarity but shouldn't be sprayed by amateurs due to the safety issues (gloves, suit and respirator aren't enough with these nasties!). The two pack auto urethanes I've tried were actually too hard and glassy for lure making, meaning that the clear coat developed cracks when a lure got slammed into a rock, stump or pontoon.

Clear Coating and Finishing

Glisten PC

This is actually a 2 pack MCU, which is kind of interesting. The advantage of this product is that the stuff isn't as sensitive to moisture until the two parts are mixed, which makes it a little easier to work with and gives it a longer shelf life. Glisten PC certainly gives a very tough, clear finish to wooden lures, but is relatively expensive and a little more hassle to work with than Etex, especially if you live in a humid environment.

Marine Varnishes

Most of these are moisture cure urethanes, so the section above on MCU's applies to most of these products too.

Epoxies

Etex is just one epoxy formulation; there are dozens available. West Systems, for example have some excellent products that you can pick up in chandlery shops and the like. Many of these have excellent clarity, set very hard and can be substituted for Etex as both a wood hardener and a clear coat.

Acrylic Lacquer

This is not the best choice for lure making, in my opinion. Acrylic lacquers are cheap and readily available, but flammable and best not inhaled. The solvent quickly removes airbrush acrylics, so you need to spray light coats to start with and then layer them up. The main problem with acrylic lacquers is that they are very soft and are easily scratched and scuffed. It doesn't take too many casts before your lure starts to look pretty shabby.

Aerosol Clears

These tend to be either acrylic lacquers and therefore have the same properties described above, or they are clear enamels. The latter are usually not UV stable, so they tend to yellow quickly and break down after a season or two.

Putting A New Spin On Lure Painting

If you've ever held a lure in one hand with a pair of long nosed pliers and tried to use a template and airbrush simultaneously using your free hand, you'll know that it's near-impossible to do a good job of painting! You'll wish you had three hands.

I have a system of jigs, clamps and drying racks that become my "third hand" when I paint lures. I've been using this system for some years now and it continues to perform very well. It includes:

- Lure clamps that grip any sized towpoint or hook hanger comfortably and hold the lures securely for dipping, spraying, applying templates and so on. There is no need to touch the actual lure at any time during painting – which means no issues with fingerprints in the paint or clear. The clamps can be moved from painting jigs in my spray booth to holding jigs in the drying area or on the rotating drying rack in just seconds.
- Cylindrical handles on the clamps allowing the lure to be rotated so I can to switch from spraying the sides to the back or belly in seconds.
- Painting jigs that hold the lure clamps stationary and securely, leaving both hands free, so I can guide the airbrush, or hold a template in one hand while I airbrush with the other.
- A rotating drying rack that takes lures on a helical motion path for perfectly even coating with epoxy or dipped finishes.
- Clamps that are compact, cheap and fast to make, so you can easily have dozens of them on hand.

The whole system can be made in a few hours for around 100 bucks, and I've put the plans and parts list at the end of this book.

What Is A Helical Motion Path And Why Is It Important?

When you are using spray cans or an airbrush, the paint should be going onto your lures in thin coats and then drying before the next coat is applied. If you're doing it right, there's no chance it will drip or run, so keeping the lures moving is not necessary.

When you apply thicker, slow drying coatings by brushing or dipping, there is a much greater chance that the paint will finish up thicker in one part of the lure, or will create a run or dag that has to be sanded off later.

The simplest way to avoid this nuisance is to hang your lures vertically and just occasionally touch the lower-most point with a piece of paper towel to draw off the drops of excess. The main problem with this approach is that the lure doesn't get evenly coated. The paint or clear slowly migrates downwards, so the coating is thicker at the bottom, as show in the diagram below.

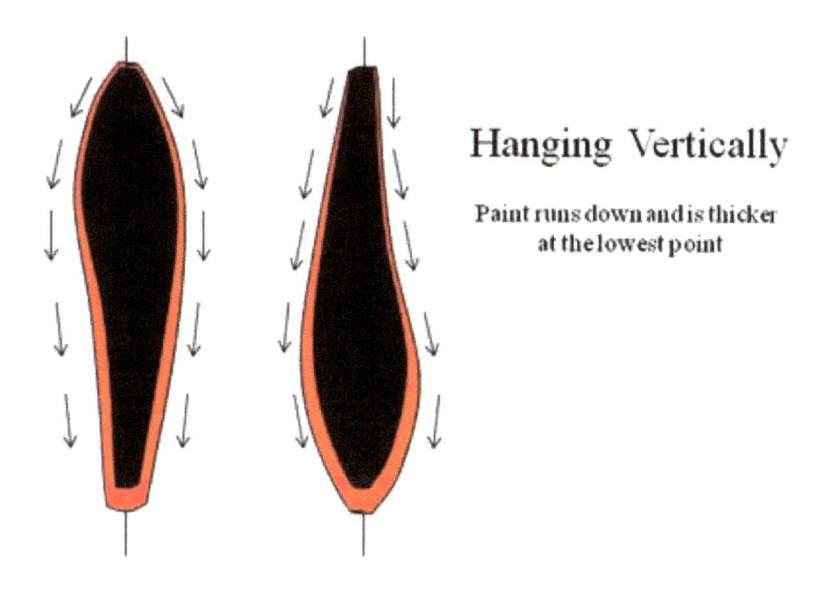

Hanging Vertically

Paint runs down and is thicker at the lowest point

Hanging your lures vertically causes dipped or brushed clear coats to be thicker at the lowest point.

Of course, you also need to keep coming back and checking on your lures or the excess will form a blob at the lowest point that has to be removed manually later.

A better option is to put the lure on some kind of rotating drying rack to keep it moving while the paint dries. Most of the lure drying racks I've seen tend to rotate in one plane only, which is better than nothing and means you don't need to be watching and blotting constantly. But the downside is that the coating still doesn't go on evenly, as shown below.

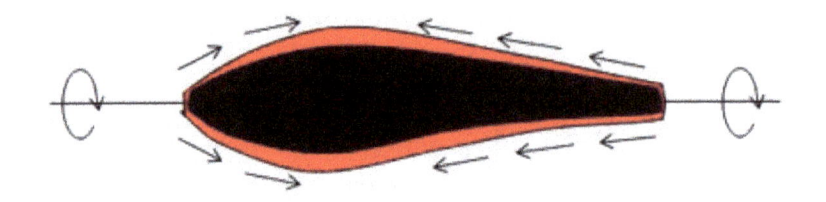

Horizontal Rolling

Paint runs and is thicker
around the middle

Rotating in one plane only is better than hanging lures, but still doesn't result in even coverage of the paint or clear coat.

In most cases it won't cause you too many problems if the coating is a little thicker around the midsections, so this type of drying rack is way ahead of the hanging kind. But if you're using very heavy coatings, like thick epoxy, it can change the weight distribution a little – and that affects the action ever so slightly.

If you want your paint or clear to lay down evenly over the lure, you need the lure to move in a helical motion, as shown in the diagram below.

Helical Motion

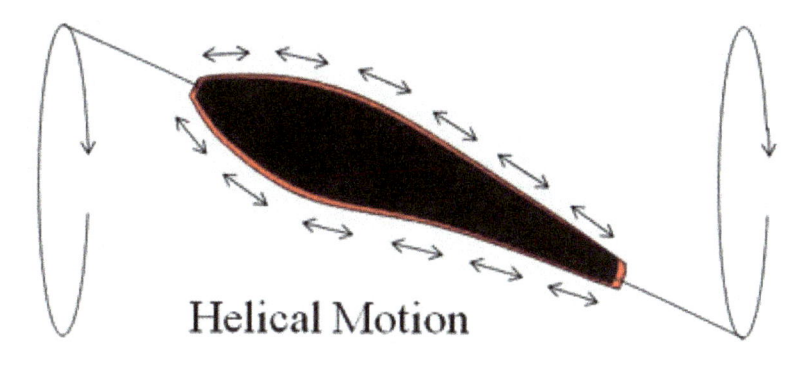

Paint spreads evenly across entire lure surface

Rotating your lures helically causes the clear coat to level out evenly over the whole lure.

It's no more difficult, time consuming or costly to make a drying rack that gives you that perfect helical motion, so why would you bother making one that doesn't?

Building A Rotating Drying Jig

Let's take an overview of my rotating drying jig so you can be familiar with the parts I've used.

We'll start by making the base, which is comprised of a backplate (1), a baseplate (2), a pair of braces (4) and a barbecue rotisserie motor (5). Then we'll make the faceplate (2), which is attached to the backplate with a lazy Suzan bearing (6) and has the lure holders (7) fitted to it.

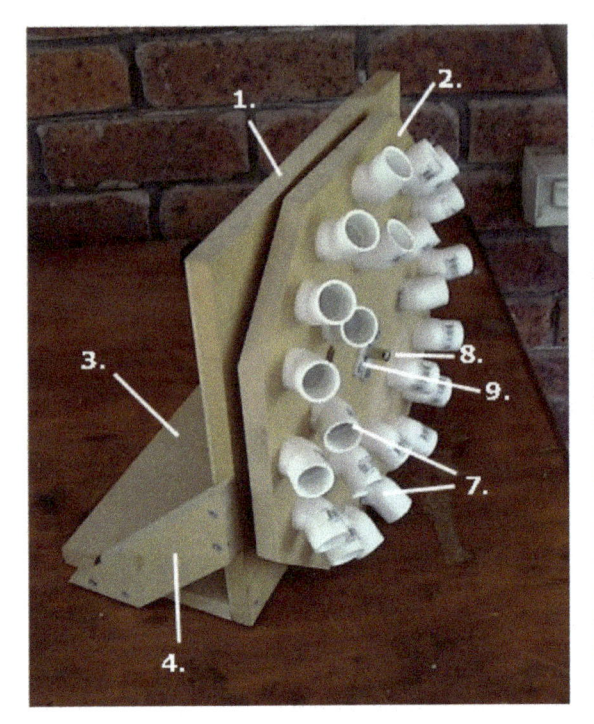

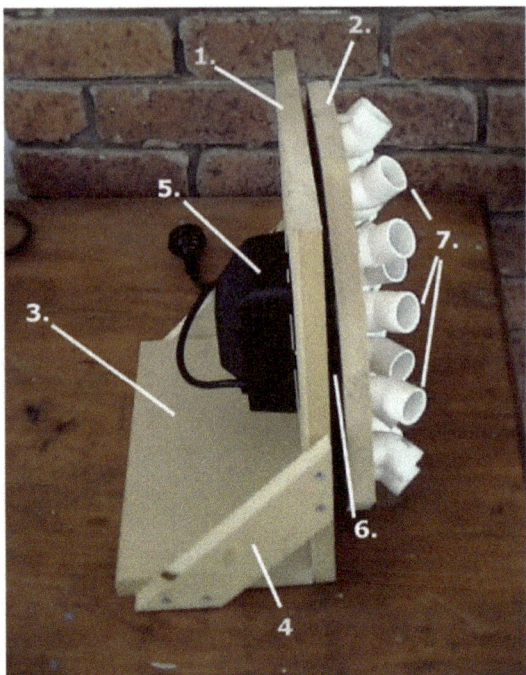

Anatomy of my rotating lure drying rack.

Building The Rotating Jig Base

The first stage in building the rotating jig is to prepare the base and fit a barbeque rotisserie motor that will drive the faceplate.

Remove the back plate from the rotisserie motor. The model I used had a pressed metal plate held to the main body of the motor by three self tapping screws. Once the screws were removed the plate came off easily and could be used as a template to mark one of the 12" x 12" (300 x 300mm) MDF pieces.

I drilled holes though the MDF and replaced the original self tapping screws with longer ones. The baseplate would then sit on one side of the MDF and the screws would reach through and anchor the rest of the rotisserie motor to the opposite side.

I marked the center on my MDF, which is where the spline from the rotisserie motor passes through. Then I centered the large hole on the rotisserie back plate and marked the location of the screw holes. These were drilled using a twist bit that gave the self-tappers a snug fit.

Removing the backplate from the rotisserie motor.

Because the rotisserie motor back plate was pressed to recess the screws, I had to drill some larger holes in the MDF so the plate could sit flat. I used a 9/16" (14mm) spade bit to drill a hole a few millimetres deep and then used the same spade bit to drill the center hole for the spline.

The rotiserrie motor backplate, ready for installation.

It was then a simple matter to fix the motor to the MDF back plate using longer self tapping screws, as shown in the photo below.

The motor installed on the back plate.

With the motor attached, I marked and drilled holes to mount a lazy Suzan bearing using woodscrews. I placed the bearing on the back plate with the main hole of the bearing aligned over the center hole of the backplate and then marked on the MDF where the screws would go.

With the back plate complete, the next step was to attach a base plate that would sit flat on my benchtop. I made this from a piece of ¾" (19mm) thick MDF, 12" x 6" (300 x 150mm) in size. I used four woodscrews to hold the two parts together, and to give it extra strength I ran a bead of white wood glue (PVA) along the edge before putting in the screws.

I used offcuts of MDF to make the braces that strengthen the connection between the back plate and the baseplate. These were ¾" (19mm) MDF, 8" long by 2" wide (200 x 50mm), with the ends cut at 45 degrees. They were glued and screwed in place, and the whole assembly was put aside while the glue dried.

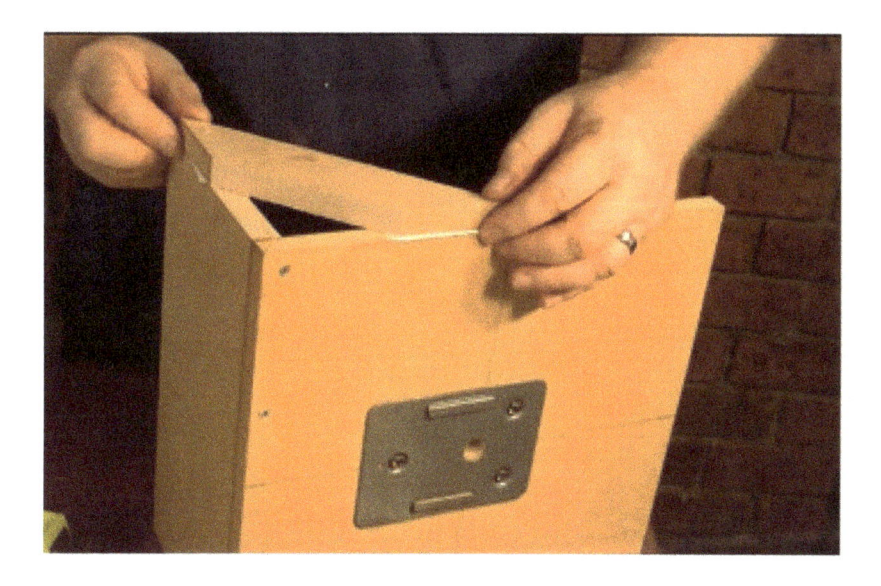

Fitting the baseplate and braces.

Building And Fitting The Faceplate

The faceplate is the part that actually holds the lures and rotates. Once again, I made mine from a 12" x 12" (300 x 300mm) piece of ¾" (18mm) MDF.

Getting Started In Custom Painted Crankbaits

I started by marking the MDF for the lure holders, which were made from 1" (20mm) high pressure PVC pipe fittings. To save drilling angled holes in the faceplate, I used 45 degree elbow fittings for this component, so the holes could instead be drilled vertically, making the process a lot easier.

I marked the center of the faceplate and marked horizontals, verticals and diagonals, giving me 8 evenly spaced lines across the front of the MDF faceplate. Then I split each of the 8 segments in two, giving me 16 lines radiating evenly from the middle of the plate.

I used a $^9/_{16}$" (14mm) drill bit to bore the center hole and laid the lazy Suzan bearing on the faceplate, marking where one of the mounting holes would be. When the faceplate was ready for mounting I would need to be able to screw the lazy Suzan bearing to the back plate so I drilled a $^9/_{16}$" (14mm) hole to facilitate screwdriver access.

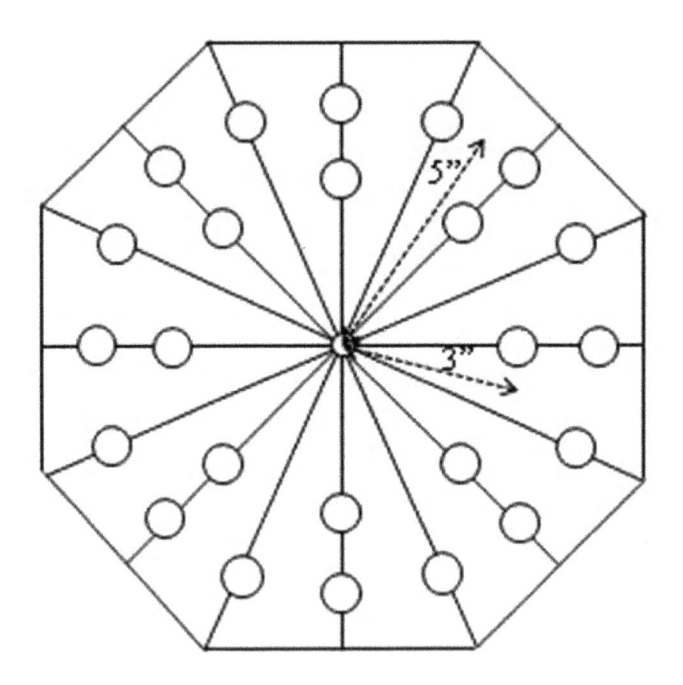

Diagram showing the layout of the faceplate.

Now it was time to drill the holes for the lure holders. I wanted to space

Putting A New Spin On Lure Painting

these out so the lures wouldn't be too close together, so I marked each line on the faceplate at a distance of 5" (125mm). Then I marked every second line at 3" (75mm) and drilled the holes for the lure holders as shown in the picture below.

I'm just telling you what I did for my own jig here – you can vary the dimensions to suit yourself. For example, making the faceplate 4" (100mm) larger in diameter would allow you to make a third row of lure holders. By splitting each of the segments in two you could add another 16 lure holders to give yourself a total capacity of 40 lures. Or you might stagger them differently and squeeze more into the same sized faceplate.

Even if you decide later that you need a bigger capacity jig, it's just a matter of making a new faceplate and switching over, which will only set you back a few bucks for some MDF and a handful more PVC elbows.

I chose to cut the corners off my faceplate at 45 degrees, giving me an octagon shaped plate. This doesn't affect the functionality of the jig, but I figured the corners might get in the way when I was putting lures on and off the jig while the motor was running. You could leave it square if you prefer, or you could even put it on the bandsaw and cut a circle.

Fitting the lazy Suzan bearing to the back of the faceplate is simply a matter of aligning the center hole and driving some wood screws through the mounting holes, so I did this before fitting the elbows.

I managed to get the holes for the lure holders snug enough that the elbow fittings could be pushed into place and didn't require any glue or screws to hold them. The outer diameter of the ¾" (20mm) elbow fittings I used is 26.6mm (a shade over 1"), so a 1" (25mm) spade bit was perfect for drilling a hole that gave a very tight fit. I used a belt sander to remove just a little plastic from the leading edge of each of the elbows to make it easier to get them into the holes initially, then just used brute force to work them deep enough into the MDF so that they were secure. Over a few years of use these have loosened a little, so I've glued them in with some epoxy now.

With the lure holders in place, the faceplate is ready to be installed on the base. To do this, I laid the base on its back and held the faceplate in place. With my battery drill fitted with a Phillips head screwdriver bit, I rotated the faceplate until the access hole I drilled was over the first mounting hole, dropped a self-tapping screw in place and drove it home. With a little manipulation, I got the next mounting hole aligned with the pilot hole in the backplate and drove in a second woodscrew. Then I drove home the final two screws to secure the mounting plate to the base.

With the faceplate fixed to the base, all that remained was to install a spline to connect the motor and faceplate. Most rotisserie motors come with a square drive, so all that's required is to find a suitable sized, square section piece of steel bar to use as a spline. For my drying jig I found that the square section bar from an old door lever was a perfect fit.

I pushed the square shaft through the faceplate and into the rotisserie motor, then screwed two flat, right angle brackets to the faceplate to form a square hole. This arrangement locks the square shaft in place and makes the faceplate turn when the motor is on.

Making Lure Painting Vices

One of the most annoying things you'll experience in lure making is to drop a lure that you've spent hours painting just before the paint has dried! All that's usually left to do is start the painting over (after much cursing)!

Locking pliers do a good job of gripping a tow point or hook hanger, which minimises such slip ups, and a fly tying vice can be quite useful too. But both have the problem that the lure has to be removed and held some other way if you want to rotate it during drying.

To maximise efficiency and minimise the number of lures that I have to repaint I designed lure vices that could hold my work while I was painting and could be transferred directly to my rotating drying rack. This means that I don't have to touch the lure with my fingers from the time I finish sanding it until the final clear coat goes on.....which saves fingerprints or oily patches where the paint doesn't lay down properly.

The design that I came up with was inspired by the forceps used by doctors and surgeons, which provide a strong but gentle grip. I made the jaws from aluminum, although steel would probably do a better job in many ways. I went with softer material because I could quickly cut a whole bunch of pieces to size

Putting A New Spin On Lure Painting

using a tungsten carbide saw blade – plus it's rust-proof!

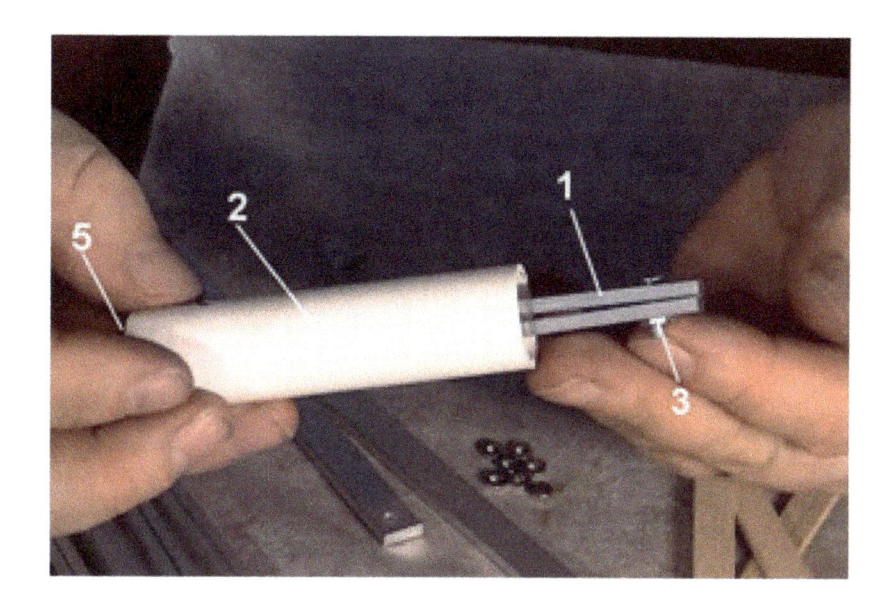

Anatomy of my lure painting clamps.

My lure vices are very simple, yet effective. A pair of aluminum jaws (1) are held together by small bolts (3) and are held in a PVC handle (2) by epoxy resin (5). A small washer (4) is not visible in the photo above but is sandwiched between the blades to create a spring effect.

I started by cutting a whole bunch of flat bar pieces that were 4 ½" (110mm) in length. On one end of each piece I drilled a hole that was 1/8" (3mm) diameter, located in the middle of the bar about 3/8" (8mm) from the end. Then I put two pieces together with a ½" (12mm) long bolt and nut and with the two pieces held together by the bolt, drilled a hole through the other end of both pieces.

I found that the trick to getting the jaws to grip the lure tightly is that there needs to be a thin metal item of some sort between the aluminum jaws to create a spring effect. I did this by loosening the bolts and slipping a thin steel washer in about 1" (25mm) from the bolt at one end (see pic below). When the closer of the two bolts is tightened, a spring effect occurs giving the business end of the vice a better grip. The washer gets held permanently in place later on when I put epoxy resin in the handle.

The handles for my vices are 2 ½" (65mm) lengths of ¾" (20mm) diameter PVC pipe. About 3/4" (19mm) from one end of the pipe I drilled a couple of 1/8" (3mm) holes to give the resin something to key into and keep it secure in the handle.

To fix the vices into the handles I worked auto body filler into the end of the PVC pipe until it was about a quarter full. Then I sat the pipe upright on a piece of oven-proof baking paper so the resin was held in the bottom while I pushed the jaws of the vice into it. The excess resin that squeezed out of the holes was worked back into the handle and I held the jaws in place for a few minutes while the resin hardened.

The holes in the end of the PVC had a slight bulge of excess resin. Just before the resin went absolutely rock hard, I scraped away the excess with my thumbnail and gave the PVC a good rub with a piece of kitchen paper that had been dampened with methylated spirits. This removed the excess resin from the surface of the handle so that there was nothing to stop the vice from sliding snugly into the lure holders on my rotating jig.

To use the lure vices, simply loosen the bolt at the end of the jaws until the opening is wide enough to take the wire or screw eyes you are using for your hook hangers. Slip the lure in and tighten the nut until the jaws have a tight grip on the wire, then use a fine screwdriver and pliers or a wrench to nip the tightness up a notch.

Putting A New Spin On Lure Painting

Setting the vice into the PVC handle using epoxy.

Lure Holding Jigs

The rotating jig and the vices are fairly simple, but the good news is that the jigs I use for holding lures during painting are even simpler and can be knocked together for a couple of bucks out of scraps and cheap components from the plumbing section of the local hardware store!

Here are some suggestions:

- Straight PVC pipe connectors can be screwed to a block of scrap MDF or lumber and are perfect for holding a lure vice for hands-free painting.
- A couple of 45 degree elbows fitted into holes in a scrap of MDF makes a great holding rack when you are working on the head end of a lure, for instance when putting on eyes.
- A piece of MDF or lumber with some 1" (25mm) holes in it is perfect for holding a whole bunch of lures vertical during drying. Lures can quickly be put in and taken out of the rack, where there is minimal chance that they'll fall or touch each other.

Getting Started In Custom Painted Crankbaits

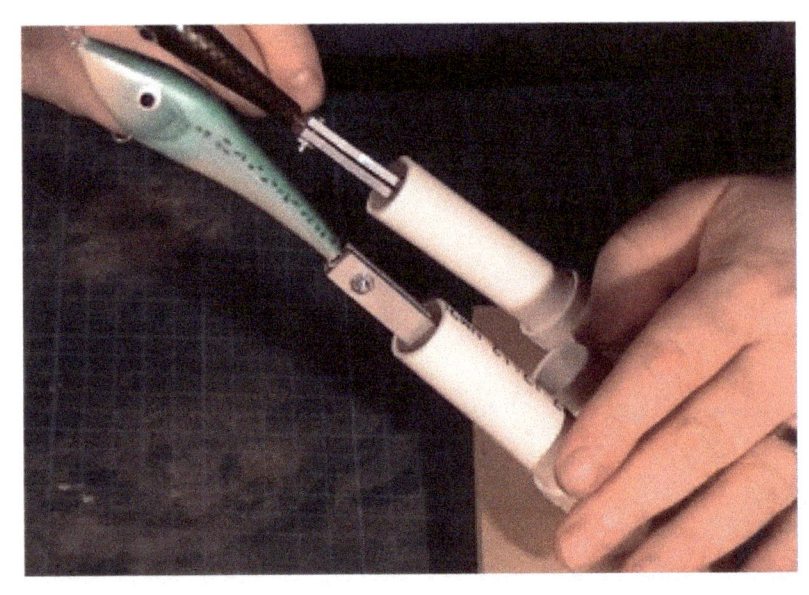

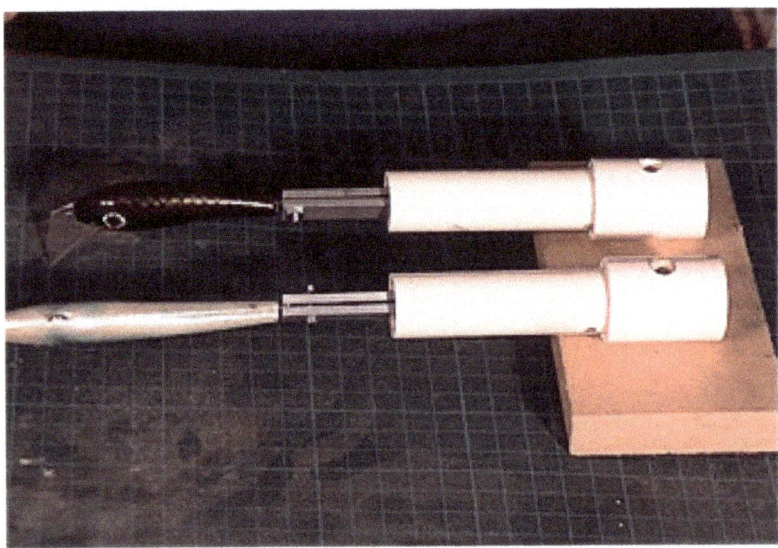

Lure holding jigs fashioned from scrap MDF and PVC fittings. These can hold the lures while you're painting them, keeping both hands free to manage the airbrush and stencils.

Airbrush Troubleshooting

This section provides generic solutions and suggestions to common airbrush painting problems. Note that I am not an airbrush guru and I'm really only familiar with those brands and models of airbrush, paint and equipment that I use in my own workshop. For more specific advice you'll need to contact your product manufacturer.

Airbrush and Equipment Issues

No Air Flow at Nozzle

- *Is the compressor on, functioning properly and the airbrush properly connected?*
  Turn on compressor and connect airbrush correctly.
- *Is the airbrush hose free of kinks and not trapped under anything heavy?*
  Remove kinks or obstructions to air flow.
- *Is the airbrush properly assembled?*
  Ensure airbrush assembled to manufacturer's specifications, check that o-rings are serviceable and all parts are clean and free of dry paint.
- *Is the small hole behind the nozzle at the front of the main body clear of paint and debris?*
  Remove paint cap and nozzle, check that the hole is clear. If blocked, soak in thinners or acetone to soften paint so that it can be blown out with compressed air.
- *Is the air valve where the hose and airbrush connect clean and free of paint?*
  If the air supply is working but air is not getting through the airbrush (assuming the flow paths are clean) it is likely that the air valve is defective. In some airbrushes this can be removed, dismantled and cleaned but in others it must be replaced.

Sticky Trigger

- *Is the trigger mechanism assembled correctly?*
  Check with manufacturer's instructions to ensure the trigger mechanism has been properly assembled. If not correct it.
- *Is there paint in or around the trigger assembly?*
  This can occur if the needle is removed while there is paint in the airbrush, or may be the result of a needle bearing or seal that is non-functional. Dismantle the trigger assembly and clean out all traces of paint using small nylon brushes and q-tips soaked in alcohol, acetone or thinners. Replace faulty parts, reassemble and lubricate with a drop or two if airbrush lubricant. Put beeswax on threads.

Paint Is Bubbling In The Color Cup

- *Is the airbrush assembled correctly, in particular, are the nozzle and head (needle cap and nozzle cap) properly seated and snug?*
  Check for correct assembly and adjust if necessary.
- *Are the nozzle and needle clean and free of dried paint?*
  Free floating nozzle (tip) must seat properly into body of airbrush. Check that it is clean, free of paint/dirt and is not obviously out of shape. To test nozzle, rub the part that seats in the main body with a little beeswax and see if this rectifies the problem. If the bubbling stops, then the nozzle requires replacement.
- *Is there a gasket near the nozzle and is it serviceable?*
  Screw in type nozzles sometimes have gaskets. If this is missing, flattened or damaged it should be replaced. If your airbrush is the type with a screw nozzle that does not have a gasket, put some beeswax in the thread and tighten carefully (extreme care not to over tighten).
- *Is the tip of the nozzle cracked, split or out of shape?*
  Hairline cracks in the nozzle can be difficult to see, so check closely. Replace the nozzle if it is defective.

Airbrush Troubleshooting

Airbrush Sprays Intermittently

- *Is the paint properly reduced?*
  Paint that is too thick can contribute to intermittent spraying, so check that first.
- *Is the airbrush assembled correctly, in particular, are the nozzle and head (needle cap and nozzle cap) properly seated and snug?*
  Check for correct assembly and correct if necessary.
- *Are the nozzle and needle clean and free of dried paint?*
  Free floating nozzle (tip) must seat properly into the body of the airbrush. Check that it is clean, free of paint/dirt and is not obviously out of shape.
- *Is there a gasket near the nozzle and is it serviceable?*
  Screw-in type nozzles sometimes have gaskets. If this is missing, flattened or damaged it should be replaced. If your airbrush is the type with screw nozzle that does not have a gasket, put some beeswax in the thread and tighten carefully (extreme care not to over tighten).
- *Is the tip of the nozzle cracked, split or out of shape?*
  Hairline cracks in the nozzle can be difficult to see, so check closely. Replace the nozzle if it is defective.
- *Is the small hole in the color cup/bottle lid blocked?*
  This can create a vacuum in the color cup, so use a fine point to clear the hole and restore air flow.

Airbrush Sprays Paint Only When Air Flow is Started or Continues Spraying When Paint is Off But Air Is On (Dual Action Airbrushes Only)

- *Is the needle and nozzle clean and free of dried paint/dirt?*
  Dismantle the airbrush and examine the needle and nozzle. Dried paint or particles of dirt can prevent the needle sealing correctly in the nozzle, so soak both parts in solvent for an hour or so and then clean them with a soft lint free cloth. While the parts are still wet with solvent, push the needle gently into the nozzle and with light pressure roll it between your fingers until it seals correctly. Rinse both parts in solvent again and reassemble the airbrush.

- *Is the needle straight and shiny?*
  A dull or dirty needle can be polished using 800-1000 grit wet/dry paper. If the needle has been polished a lot it may be out of shape and require replacement. Likewise, if it is bent it should be replaced.
- *Is the nozzle round, free of splits and correctly shaped?*
  Check the condition of the nozzle, if it is no longer serviceable then replace it.

Airbrush Gets Air Flow But Not Paint

- *Has the paint been correctly thinned with reducer and filtered to remove lumps and/or debris?*
  Paint that is too thick or contains particles or impurities can block the nozzle. This is preventable by properly reducing and filtering the paint before use. If the nozzle has become blocked it may be necessary to dismantle the airbrush and soak the nozzle in solvent for a while. Then gently push the needle into the nozzle and rotate it between your finger and thumb. Remove it and wipe off any paint. Reassemble the airbrush and recommence painting.
- *Is the needle able to slide in the needle chuck?*
  If the needle isn't held securely by the chuck it may not be moving when you push the trigger. Tightening the chuck will fix this problem. If the needle is sliding in the chuck because it has become jammed by dried up paint you will need to strip the airbrush down and soak the key parts in solvent until the paint softens and can be cleaned out.
- *Is the small hole in the color cup/bottle lid blocked?*
  This can create a vacuum in the color cup, so use a fine point to clear the hole and restore air flow.
- *Is the seal between the color pot and airbrush airtight (siphon feed airbrush only)?*
  Test the airbrush by removing the color cup, turning the airbrush upside down and putting some water in the paint inlet. If the airbrush works in this position it is likely that the seal for the siphon feed needs attention.

Airbrush Troubleshooting

Air Hose Leaks

- *Can you hear hissing at either end of the air hose?*
  Hoses rarely split. Leaks are most common at the connections. Brush soapy water on the connections between the hose and the compressor/airbrush. If there is a leak you will see bubbles form. Depending on the brand of equipment you are using it may be a case of replacing cork/Teflon washers or an o-ring. Teflon tape or beeswax on the threads may also help improve the seal. If not, replace the hose.

Issues With Paint/Spray Pattern

Paint Has Grainy ("Orange Peel") Appearance

The grainy appearance in paint is generally caused by paint partially drying between the airbrush and the lure. Possible solutions:

- Reduce air pressure
- Hold airbrush closer to the lure
- Reduce the paint more
- Use a slower drying reducer

Paint Has A Coarse Or Speckled Appearance

Usually caused by poor atomisation of the paint. Possible solutions:

- Increase air pressure
- Thin the paint more
- Ensure trigger is fully depressed during painting

Paint Drying On Tip Of Needle

Common problems with acrylic paints drying on the tip of the needle is due to its fast drying times. To some extent, we just have to accept this as part of airbrushing with this paint system and be prepared to clean the tip of the needle from time to time using a q-tip soaked in solvent. Other things to try include:

- Reduce the paint a little more
- Reduce air pressure
- Using slower drying reducer, or add acrylic retarder to the paint

Paint "Spiders" (Ball With Lines Coming From It)

Paint spiders are usually caused when paint flow is started while the airbrush is not moving, but can sometimes be due to a damaged nozzle, tip or needle. Possible solutions:

- Ensure that the airbrush is not stationary when the paint flow starts or ends
- Check the nozzle for splits and other damage, and replace if necessary
- Check that the needle is not bent, and repair or replace if necessary

Paint "Spatters"

Paint spatters are a common problem with single action airbrushes, especially when the flow first starts and when it finishes. Possible solutions:

- Ensure that the airbrush is not pointed at your lure when you start or stop the paint flow.
- Try cleaning the airbrush thoroughly, removing and draining the hose or installing a water trap.
- Try thinning the paint more and/or increase the air pressure.
- A worn or damaged nozzle or needle can contribute to paint spatter. Check these and replace if necessary.

Airbrush Troubleshooting

Sometimes with dual action airbrushes spatter occurs as a result of poor technique, rather than an actual fault with the airbrush. The following measures usually sort the problem out:

- The trigger should be fully depressed during painting. If you need to increase or decrease airflow it should be done with the regulator, not the airbrush.
- Keep the air flowing between bursts of painting, this will stop paint from accumulating at the tip and will reduce spatter and minimize dry paint on the tip.
- Ensure that the trigger is fully depressed before pulling back to start the paint flow. When stopping, make sure paint is fully stopped before releasing trigger to stop the airflow.
- Try to point the airbrush away from your lure when you are starting airflow or paint flow (not always possible).
- Avoid snapping the trigger closed or opening it suddenly while the airbrush is pointed at your lure.

Metallic Paints Block Airbrush

Blockages are a common problem with metallic paints not formulated for airbrushes, but can also happen when airbrush paints are used incorrectly. It's often the result of metallic flake being too big to pass through the airbrush nozzle. Possible solutions:

- Stick with metallics formulated for use with airbrushes.
- Reduce metallic paint slightly more than standard paint.
- Increase pressure to push the flake through the airbrush.
- Ensure nozzle size is sufficient to handle metallics. 0.3mm seems to be the minimum nozzle size, from what I've seen and heard. I have no trouble shooting AutoAir metallics through the 0.3mm nozzle of my Iwata HP- CS.
- Another option that seems to work is to thin the paint a little more and then reduce the air pressure. This allows you to pull the trigger back further to get the same paint delivery, which opens the nozzle right up. You'll need to spray a lot of light coats and keep shaking the airbrush to keep the flake suspended.

Paints Don't Lay Down Evenly - Blotchy Appearance

Particularly problematic with metallics and pearls, but can happen with any paint. Paints not laying down evenly is usually the result of too much paint in a single pass, particularly if the paint is over reduced or the air pressure is too high. Possible solutions:

- Increase the paint to reducer ratio, reduce the air pressure and/or hold the airbrush further away from the lure.
- I always find that after a color change the first coat or two needs to be very lightly misted on, subsequent coats can be normal spray pattern. Not sure why this works, it just does!
- Build color with lots of light coats and allow the paint to dry properly between coats, preferably heat setting with a hair dryer.

Paints not laying down evenly can also be the result of oils or waxes on the surface. Possible solutions:

- Clean unpainted surface with a mild solvent, such as alcohol, prior to painting.
- Avoid touching the surface of the lure before painting and between coats of paint.

Unable To Paint Fine Lines, Small Spots

This can be a tricky issue to resolve and it takes a lot of patience and practice to get consistent fine lines and small spots. Possible solutions:

- Practice, practice, practice!
- Use really thin paint and keep the airbrush very close to the lure.
- Use minimum air pressure to get good atomisation of the paint (5 PSI).
- Remove the needle cap (but be careful not to damage needle).
- Don't do this with metallics, pearls etc. Best coverage comes from using darker opaque paints, but transparent paints can give good results too.

Airbrush Troubleshooting

Poor Spray Pattern

Spray pattern may be split, double lined, uneven, spraying to one side etc. Possible solution:

- Usually the result of a damaged nozzle/tip and/or needle. Check, clean, repair and replace if necessary.

Other Wooden Lure Making Resources

Other Lure Making Resources From Greg "Doc Lures" Vinall:

- Make Wooden Lures (http://makewoodenlures.com) is a site packed with information and tips for wooden lure makers.
- Make Your Own Lures: Wooden Lures (2nd Edition) is an eBook that goes through the essentials of wooden lure making in a logical, step by step way. Available from the Wooden Lure Workshop website http://woodenlureworkshop.com.
- The Crankbait Masterclass is an online wooden lure making course that takes participants through some of the most advanced techniques around.... and makes them simple! http://thecrankbaitmasterclass.com.
- "Why fish don't see your lures" is a kindle eBook that takes an indepth look at how lure color selection can affect your fishing results.

Stay in touch with Greg on Facebook:

http://facebook.com/woodenluremaking

CPSIA information can be obtained
at www.ICGtesting.com
Printed in the USA
BVHW022058140620
581479BV00002B/36